bear season

bear season

a journey

into

Ursidae

KATHERINE AYRES

Autumn House
Press

pittsburgh

"Autumn House" and "Autumn House Press" are registered trademarks
owned by Autumn House Press, a nonprofit corporation whose mission
is the publication and promotion of poetry and other fine literature.

Autumn House Press Staff
Editor-in-Chief and Founder: Michael Simms
Managing Editor: Giuliana Certo
Production Editor: Caroline Tanski
Assistant Editor: Christine Stroud
Interns: Heather Cazad, Noah Gup
Co-Founder: Eva-Maria Simms
Community Outreach Director: Michael Wurster
Fiction Editors: Sharon Dilworth, John Fried
Media Consultant: Jan Beatty
Tech Crew Chief: Michael Milberger

PENNSYLVANIA
COUNCIL
ON THE

ARTS

Autumn House Press receives state arts funding support through a
grant from the Pennsylvania Council on the Arts, a state agency funded
by the Commonwealth of Pennsylvania, and the National Endowment
for the Arts, a federal agency.

ISBN: 978-1-932870-90-9
Library of Congress Control Number: 2013942914

All Autumn House books are printed on acid-free paper and meet the international standards
for permanent books intended for purchase by libraries.

☆

Bears are not companions of men, but children of God. . . .
A bear's days are warmed by the same sun, his dwellings
are overdomed by the same blue sky, and his life turns and
ebbs with heart-pulsings like ours and was poured from
the same fountain . . .

—John Muir

☆

for my mother
and for mothers everywhere

contents

introduction

SUDDENLY and seemingly out of nowhere, I find myself obsessed with bears. And when something like that happens I usually spend a lengthy spell at the keyboard, ignoring pressing deadlines, lunch, my family. And then piles upon piles of paper, a cluttered desk, an impassible office. Midnight trips to the computer to add one more interesting fact, one more witty quip.

I'm pleased to discover that I'm not the only one. The following musing has circulated widely on the web since at least 2007, author unknown:

> In this life I'm a woman. In my next life, I'd like to come back as a bear. When you're a bear, you get to hibernate. You do nothing but sleep for six months. I could deal with that.
>
> Before you hibernate, you're supposed to eat yourself stupid. I could deal with that too.
>
> When you're a girl bear, you birth your children (who are the size of walnuts) while you're sleeping and wake to partially grown, cute, cuddly cubs. I could definitely deal with that.
>
> If you're mama bear, everyone knows you mean business. You swat anyone who bothers your cubs. If your cubs get out of line, you swat them too. I could deal with that.
>
> If you're a bear, your mate EXPECTS you to wake up growling. He EXPECTS that you will have hairy legs and excess body fat.
>
> Yup, gonna be a bear!

This writer feels like a sister. Her words cheer me on as I embark on this journey into *Ursidae*, the family of the bears.

bear season

☆

The mountains have always been here, and in them, the bears.

—Rick Bass

☆

protection

SEVEN O'CLOCK AND I stand at the sink washing up from my solitary supper—chili from the big pot in the fridge. Out the window a large black bear, *Ursus americanus,* ambles past, then rears up on her hind legs halfway between the house and the pin oak, *Quercus palustris,* a mere ten feet from where I stand. She drops down, loping along on four feet but still impressive. Her shaggy black coat shines in the light of the low hanging sun.

I freeze and watch until she wanders out of sight, dry my hands and hurry to the sun porch to continue my vigil. She doesn't hurry —it seems as if she's strolling home after a hard day at work, which may be the case. In Massachusetts, in June, her summer job is to eat, nonstop, and build up fat layers decimated by months of hibernation.

I call her *she,* but I really don't know. Perhaps this bear is male. Bears have such thick fur that at a distance, it's hard to identify gender, even when they stand upright. Females tend to have narrower, more pointed faces than males, but with only one bear to observe, I can't make comparisons.

At this moment, she is solitary as I am solitary. No cubs or offspring nearby, which might mark the bear as a male, but I doubt it somehow. She has a large and well-developed body, but not hulking.

Female black bears range from 100 to 400 pounds; males from 130 to 600. If I had to guess for this bear, I'd estimate a weight on the leaner side, perhaps 200, so I choose to think of her as *she*. She is my third bear.

☆

I saw my first bear at age ten, riding in a car at night with my parents, great-grandmother and a great-uncle. We were driving a dark, narrow, forested park road near Blackwater Falls, deep in the hills of West Virginia. A campground scavenger, a Dumpster bear, most likely, it crossed the road and we caught its shape in the headlights, stopped, watched its passage. Seeing a bear in the wild, close-up, thrilled me. Then as now, layers of protection shielded me—the heavy steel of our car, its thick windows, and chiefly my parents, whom I knew would guard me from all danger, forever and ever.

My great-grandmother died a few years later when I was a teenager. My great-uncle many years beyond that. My parents live on in their eighties, in relative good health for their time of life. I am one of a handful of friends and acquaintances who still can claim an intact family of origin: my mother, my father, myself. I can still claim the name, *child*. Though other family names have attached themselves to me as time has passed—wife, mother, and now grandmother—none but child have stretched across my entire life, forever and ever.

Change is coming; if I watch, I catch its shape in the headlights. My father-in-law has entered the no-man's-land of Alzheimer's. My parents live in a community of elders and among their friends I see troubling signs: the slower locomotion, the fast forgetting, the shoulders that dip and sag.

I wonder about that name, *child*. Having both parents might imply a certain immaturity. While I cherish a youthful attitude, I sometimes feel frivolous, self-indulgent, allowed to skip along lightly because the rock upon which my life was built still stands. And like a child, at times I want to scrunch my eyes tight, to deny the future, to refuse to see.

Early on, before adolescence hit and I needed to rush forward into LIFE, a part of me did not wish to grow up at all. At eight, nine, ten, I loved my life. I got to play, to spend endless days outside in the sun. To run—run down and down to the creek at the very bottom of the hill. Or to climb, up to the very top of the apple tree and hide among its soft, dusty leaves. Adult lives seemed boring, filled with worry and work. Whoever would want to give up the world of childhood? Not I.

☆

My second bear came on a camping trip, with no layers of steel or glass to protect me. Just myself and my then-husband. We sat by our two-man, orange tent in Jasper Park, Alberta, fiddling around the campfire. He perched on a log with a small hatchet and chopped kindling. Across the clearing, I scrubbed up the pot we'd used to cook our evening meal.

At first, it appeared to be a large black dog. Then as it lumbered closer—bear. I froze and so did my husband. The bear sniffed the perimeter of our tent but didn't claw through. We'd been told not to store or eat any food in the tent and we'd listened. No midnight snacks.

The bear studied us from the far side of the fire—but not far enough for me. He could have been on us in three strides. We made up a sort of equilateral triangle—man—woman—bear—an unmoving diorama. Finally he turned away, crunching leaves and branches underfoot as he went.

"Thank goodness you had the hatchet," I said, once I could breathe again.

"Are you crazy?" came the reply. "This little hatchet and that big bear? You could have saved us. All you had to do was bang that stupid pot and scare it away." So much for protection.

That bear, or a close acquaintance, came back early the next morning, but not to our tent. We heard the distinctive crash of branches that warns of something large nearby. Then the swearing began.

We unzipped the flap and peeked out to see a guy in the next tent scrambling out, pulling up his jeans as he went. Barefoot, he chased after, yelling. "Give me back my food, you damn bear. That's *my* food sack." We stepped out of our tent to watch and snap photos; so did several other campers.

The guy must have made enough noise to worry the bear, because he came back with a torn nylon food sack in hand, still muttering, "Damn bear."

He clambered up the nearby tree and removed the rest of his supplies, which he'd hung on a broken-off branch. The Canadian kids we'd met while traveling had a better strategy. They rigged a bear line up between two trees, threaded their food bags on the line and hoisted them high in the air. Out of reach.

"Damn bear. Ripped my sack. Spilled most of my milk."

Damn fool, I thought.

☆

Biologists classify bears as *Caniforms,* large dog-like omnivores. No wonder I perceived bear number two as a big old dog. When down on all fours, they remind me of Newfoundlands with the thick black fur, the robust, sturdy bodies, the pointed muzzles.

The name *bear,* from the Old English *bera,* seems to be related to a family of names in Germanic languages, all of which mean brown. In Scandinavia, they call a bear *bjorn,* but they also call a lot of tall blond men by that name, as well as a brand of comfortable shoes. And a Welsh bear goes by *art,* which seems fitting for the homeland of King Arthur, certainly a towering, majestic presence.

Until about the 1940s and 50s, Americans considered black bears varmints—agricultural nuisances in most parts of their range. The bears preyed on small domestic animals and foraged extensively in cornfields, eating ripe ears and flattening stalks, so farmers routinely hunted and destroyed them. In 1952 Massachusetts began regulating bear hunting and protecting the species. As a result of this develop-

ment, changes in forest structure, and the wider availability of supplemental fall foods, the bear population in the state has grown from
about 100 animals in the early 1970s to about 3000 in 2005, most
living west of the Connecticut River as I do.

During each of the past ten years, about half of the bears harvested during hunting season were killed in my county, Berkshire
County, a mostly mountainous terrain at the farthest western edge
of the state. With the exception of nuisance bears—those who threaten
humans or repeatedly invade properties—bears can only be taken
during either 17 days in September or 18 days in November. During
the rest of the year, our laws guard them from human predation. Odd,
when I think about it. We humans protect these large, magnificent
giants of the forest so we'll have more of them to hunt and kill.

☆

I press closer to the window. This bear, my third bear, crosses the
lawn, my lawn, and angles toward the cottage in back, still moving
slowly, casually. And why not? Not a lot of woods creatures will tangle with a full-grown black bear, and June means mating season, not
hunting season.

I feel safe enough, inside my house. Again as in childhood, I have
protection—layers of wood, and glass, and eighteen inches of concrete between myself and the wildness that surrounds me. And so I
watch until she crosses the back driveway and pushes into the woods.
Even after she disappears, I continue to stare. A bear in my yard, the
first I've seen here, although I've heard plenty of stories. I've even
done some web-searching just in case—to be prepared. And then I
wonder if indeed it is a bear in *my yard*. Bears are territorial. They
mark their lands by rubbing their bodies against tree trunks and by
biting or gouging out long scratches in the trees' bark. The bear with
the highest teeth- or claw-marks wins the dominance battle.

I reconsider what I've just seen. This bear easily stands a foot taller
than I am. Her marks will rise much higher than I could ever reach,

should I choose to scratch at a tree trunk with my thin, puny finger-nails or nip at some bark with my own teeth.

So perhaps she has a woman in *her yard*. Perhaps she's caught my scent with that sensitive nose of hers and wonders who and why. She may believe that a stranger has invaded her territory here in the mountains of western Massachusetts and wonder if the stranger presents a threat. If it carries a rifle, bow and arrows, if it's male or female, if she needs to be vigilant, if *she* needs protection.

The wilderness is not a renewable resource. If it is possible for humans and wildlife to coexist, we must endeavor to understand as much as possible about their needs . . .

—Stephen Herrero

bear candy

"Hey, look out the window," my husband calls from upstairs. "There's a big bear in the side yard." I hear it in his voice, excitement. As I was alone in the house when the bear visited last June he hadn't yet seen her. Although we've been married for many years, we haven't shared the same sorts of outdoor experience that I knew in my first partnership. We've been more pampered, more luxurious, and of course, older. Up until this moment we haven't shared a bear sighting.

I rush to the sun porch and sure enough a large black bear is making her way purposefully from the road out front toward the wetlands behind our house and gardens. She appears to be the same size as last summer's bear and she travels in the same intentional, deliberate manner. No hurrying but no wasted movements either.

Once she enters the wetlands I race upstairs with binoculars, to the back windows with the best views.

My husband stands there, peering out into a beautiful morning. "Hurry, you'll miss this," he says.

I pass him the field glasses and join him at the window as the bear enters the wetlands and begins to graze, a patch of rippling darkness amidst the rich, pungent greens of early summer.

☆

We bought this property as our third child neared the end of college —when we no longer had huge tuition bills looming, but while we were still conditioned to paying them. We had two rationales: to get a head start on the purchase of a retirement destination for down the road; and to establish a place in a lovely setting where our mostly grown family could enjoy time together.

We were impetuous. No sooner had we decided *the Berkshires* than we made late summer plane reservations, grabbed one of the last two available B & B rooms in the county and headed east to New England. After five days in Western Massachusetts, we returned with a signed contract to purchase a large white clapboard house with a charming guest cottage sitting on four acres surrounded by wetlands and forest. Then the fun began.

When you move from house to house, you have belongings to pack, sorting and discarding to accomplish. When you buy a second home, you have none of the above. We didn't have a spoon to carry to the new house, not a pillow. I spent September through December going to auctions, house sales and consignment shops, a pastime I learned from my father. I went to auctions with him as a small child and always came home with treasures—that twenty-five cent box of kitchen gear, a strainer, spoons, a cupcake tin to use in the sandbox.

For this house, I needed more than dented bakeware. As I stitched curtains and comforters I applied simple rules: cheap, clean, sturdy. For the place to work as a second home it needed to be casual and not something that required protection. Random glassware, fine; if somebody drops a wine glass, no problem. Second-hand tables, great; nobody will notice the new scratches. My parents were downsizing, so I bought up their extras, many of which were also auction finds. When we signed papers the following January, the house sucked up everything I'd found—a 31 foot U-Haul load carried in through the snow—and still it felt empty. In the months and years since the purchase, we've gradually filled it, spruced it up.

"Masters of regional arbitrage," my husband declares. "We buy stuff for the house in the aging city of Pittsburgh where auctions and estate sales abound and make the costs modest, then carry them to New England, land of antiques, land of New York prices."

Gradually, I've also discovered a third unexpected benefit from owning a second home in the country, not something I'd anticipated. Solitude. In my city life, I'm busy: teaching graduate students; writing and rewriting books; visiting schools as author in residence; and generally participating in the urban community that surrounds me. Mostly, I love the bustle. It feels productive.

The first summer, when I spent the weeks between Memorial Day and the Fourth of July at the property, painting and gardening and generally making the place livable, I struggled with the quiet. As a newcomer, I knew nobody. My husband only flew in on alternate weekends, leaving me, an extrovert, with no one to talk to. We'd decided ahead of time no TV, so no noise, no other human voices broke the silences. That first summer, I was lonely, and as those visiting weekends approached, I grew more than a little squirrely.

Each year, I keep coming for the same span of time. We have much to accomplish. My schedule is maximally flexible once the spring semester finishes, so I am elected as chief muscle. I roll my loneliness from paint cans onto drab walls, making them glow—*lemon sorbet, rose parade*. I tear out old dank carpets and scrub the oak floor underneath, imagining the visitors who will stay in this room. I dig my quietude into rich black earth and make friends at the nearby garden center. I also get to know a couple of neighbors and lots of workmen: plumbers, electricians, lawn guys, and exterior painters. In the process, the emptiness fills with life.

☆

In my real life, I am not a morning person. These days, at the eastern edge of the time zone, I find myself waking early—those raucous birds —leaving my watch on the dresser, adjusting to a different life tempo. I work outdoors mornings, and when the sun gets too hot, switch to the indoors and write, read or putter. In the evening I watch the sky, first a sunset, then black trees dancing against a lit-from-behind, Maxfield Parrish blue. Later, I fall asleep to the frog chorus—a harmony of bullfrogs, *Rana catesbeiana,* and spring peepers, *Pseudacris crucifer.* When the squirrely moments come, I get out among people, if only at the grocery store.

As time passes, I discover a new sort of balance—long spells of solitude, interspersed with gatherings of friends and family, which seems just about perfect. The house and its land become a place of respite—a place that soothes my spirit. Now, though certainly not a hermit, I sometimes must remind myself to be sociable, to play with and share the place with others.

Occasionally, as on this particular Memorial Day weekend, I feel guilty that I can spend so much time here while my husband only comes and goes for weekends. So I too am glad he's finally seeing this bear.

☆

She would be a hard show to miss today, unless we weren't at home. In late May the skunk cabbage, *Symplocarpus foetidus,* grows bright green, all new leaves and tender shoots. It spreads in countless clumps and patches throughout the broad expanse of wetland that stretches behind us all the way to the mountain. It's an odd plant, for much of the growth hides underwater in swampy areas in early spring where the water stays warmer than the surrounding air. It sends up flowers first, then leaves and stems, once the air warms enough that the tender foliage won't freeze. Underwater a tangled mat of roots grows thick and heavy.

Skunk cabbage is bear candy, or so we've been told. This bear makes us believe it. She steps from plant to plant, grazing, shearing, devouring. She takes her time, seems committed to harvesting the entire crop that nature has provided for her. Such lush, emergent spring growth plus leftover nuts from the previous autumn nourish a bear emerging from hibernation. She will have consumed 25-40% of her body weight during the five winter months of relative inactivity. She needs all the skunk cabbage she can find.

In my opinion, she can have it. There's a reason they call it skunk cabbage. The flowers carry a particularly heavy dose of eau-de-polecat just waiting for the unsuspecting gardener or hiker to step down and crush, releasing the pungent perfume. Time for new boots.

Foot odor has nothing to boast of when compared to skunk or skunk cabbage. The stuff is filled with mercaptans, a term derived from the Latin *mercurium captans* (capturing mercury). I know the word for this strongly scented group of compounds because my first husband was an organic chemist. Another researcher in his graduate school lab was studying mercaptans and had a spill. Everyone went home that day reeking. It's not an odor one forgets.

Mercaptans, also known as thiols, contain sulphur which produces such strong odors as rotten egg or garlic. In other words they stink, like the dead skunk, *Mephitis mephitis,* lying in the center of the highway, like the scat creatures leave behind.

So now, my bear has bad breath. (Yes, she's now *my bear,* not *the bear*.) And I doubt there's a bear equivalent of Listerine or even Crest. So I'll keep my distance. I would have done that anyway. I don't intend to place myself between a large hungry omnivore and her favorite salad.

As she slogs along from plant to plant, I consider other scents and odors. While she gets partly wet in the soggy terrain, I doubt she bathes too often. With all that dark fur, she's in danger of overheating on a hot, sunny day and therefore spends a lot of her time in the shade. Smart bear. I wonder if she sweats. Like a dog, she will pant to cool off. If it gets really hot she'll dunk herself in a pond or creek, just as I will. So what does a bear smell like? I won't get close enough to discover that first hand either but I do ponder such nonsense.

For now, we just watch her—fifteen minutes and then thirty, as she feasts, as she gorges herself on this warm, bright summer morning. Finally, seemingly sated, she enters the woods and disappears from sight.

Skunk cabbage, bear candy. Makes me wonder if she's ever tasted chocolate.

*When a pine needle falls in the forest, the eagle sees it; the
deer hears it, and the bear smells it.*

—an old First Nations saying

☆

scented

I WAKE TO a light that shimmers gold-green, a Robert Frost sort
of hue. The pines, *Pinus,* have opened their primordial flowers and
drenched the world in pollen—plant sperm. Every surface indoors
and out glows pale green, phosphorescent. The pollen will stay, float-
ing in the air, coating plants and cars and houses, until rain comes to
wash it away.

I kneel in damp grass at the edge of a rectangular garden near
the creek and savor the scents of new growth, moist soil. I plant not
greenery but baked clay, a row of found bricks discovered in a pile in
the woods along with some cut stone and paving blocks, all leftovers
from the building of our house years and years ago. I want these
bricks to act as a barrier to the grasses and wild creeping buttercups,
Ranunculus repens, that keep trying to invade the Knockout roses, *Rosa
Radrazz,* and catmint, *Nepeta cataria.* While the bricks won't stop the
weeds, they may slow things down.

By the time I've finished that garden, I've earned myself some
lunch, so I grab a tuna sandwich, and then proceed to the oaks. We
have two large pin oaks in our yard—one grows along the side of the
house and one behind the sun porch. On a garden tour, I'd seen an
impressive planting—a growth of climbing hydrangea, *Hydrangea*

13

anomala ssp. petiolaris, gorgeous in full flower wrapping the trunk of a large old pine. As we had a mature hydrangea specimen beside the back door already, I could easily pull some rooted cuttings and plant them at the base of each pin oak.

Unfortunately, the lawn guy's weed-whacker keeps decapitating the fledgling plants, so we need help. I decide to plant circles of large-leaf *Hosta,* also known as *Funkia,* to protect the hydrangea vines and to crowd out the weeds that otherwise sprout around the oak trunks.

As a gardener with many new gardens planned for this old, somewhat neglected yard, I believe in short cuts. Rather than weed and cultivate, I prefer to plant, then surround the new specimen with layers of newspaper or cardboard, and mulch heavily. This forms a barrier to weeds—they get no light—and it works surprisingly well. As the plants mature and the organic material rots down, the plants themselves crowd out most of the weeds. All this adds up to more time for planting new gardens instead of endlessly tending the existing ones.

I'm sitting on the warm grass, with about four new hostas in the ground, Butter and Sage, which, as the name implies, have broad gray-green leaves edged in pale gold. I've tucked in these four new babies, watered them, and surrounded them by cardboard and mulch when I catch motion in my peripheral vision, over beyond the creek. Then a splash and a large black dog—no, my bear—stands on my side of the creek where she rears up on her hind legs and looks about.

She appears large, shaggy, and heavy, easily two hundred pounds, and nearly six feet tall standing upright. And while black bears in the west commonly wear brown, chocolate, cinnamon, honey, even ivory colored fur, this one is an Eastern Black Bear, *Ursus americanus americanus,* truly black from her small round ears to her five-toed feet.

Look large. Make noise. Don't run. Don't turn your back or you will turn into a prey animal. Never, never climb a tree for a she-bear will hide her cubs in a white pine for safety. The trees belong to the bears.

I have checked various bear safety information sources and so I rise slowly and thrust my arms out at my sides to make myself seem imposing. I don't shout because I'm not sure if she's spotted me yet. If she doesn't know I'm out here, I don't want to call attention to myself.

The bear drops down and snuffles the edge of the garden—the very spot where I'd been planting bricks an hour earlier. She sniffs the entire long edge and I know she has caught my scent.

Still looking as large as a five-foot woman can, more round than tall with arms extended, I edge slowly away from the oak tree and step backwards up the slope to the paved patio.

The bear finishes sniffing at the creek and moves toward the driveway a good twenty-five feet closer to me.

I glide across the bluestone and reach for the patio door. Slip inside. Close and lock behind me.

I'm still standing there when the phone rings. I grab for it. The plumber, talking schedules.

"Give me a minute," I explain, still catching my breath. "I was just outside and a big bear came into the yard. Pretty close."

"Cool," the guy says. "Did you get a picture?"

A picture? My hands shake so badly, any picture would show only ripples.

We sort out the schedule and I continue to watch my bear. She makes her way along the drive and passes in front of the cottage that sits back near the wetlands, a distance behind the main house. Near the edge of the woods, she stops to swat at a woven rattan papasan chair-swing that my neighbor has hung from a scotch pine, *Pinus sylvestris.* The chair swings gently and the bear watches, as if she's done this many, many times. Then she meanders off to who knows where.

I sit for a while to calm my trembling body. Then I step back outside to gather tools and tidy my mess. No more planting today. In fact, I decide to work only close to the house for the next few days, pruning overgrown shrubs, *Rhododendron ponticum,* whose huge, pink blooms are just finishing. I'll unlock all the exterior doors in case I get another visit—I'll want lots of escape strategies. I'll wait until my older daughter arrives to venture farther from the safety of the house. And even then, with two of us out, we'll both wear whistles.

All these plans calm me and I retreat to the shower, intent on a clean, indoor afternoon. By dinnertime, I've grown mellow enough to begin calling this an adventure, in spite of the fact that I'm at the house alone without a soul nearby to offer assistance in such dicey moments.

☆

I'm sitting on the patio after dinner, a glass of white wine in hand, when a dark shape again appears in my peripheral vision. The same bear, I'm pretty sure, crossing the creek in the exact same spot. She repeats every action of the afternoon, sniffing the edge of the creek garden, coming up to the driveway, then following it to the cottage.

This time I sit close to the house, feel safer, so I run in for the camera and return to shoot pictures. I grab a whistle to see if it works. Once I've shot several poses, I try the whistle, giving three long, loud blasts.

My bear doesn't even look up. She just keeps walking slowly toward the cottage, crosses in front, bats at the papasan chair, watches and disappears. That papasan—either it's a bear piñata, or she's grumpy that it's not her size. Perhaps it's just a toy.

I'm proud of myself for being brave this time—for staying outside —but am also unnerved. The whistle proved useless and I think about what else I can carry to make noise. The car keys with the car alarm button might work. If I get really scared, I can hop in the car and drive off.

But I still feel unsettled. So I phone my younger daughter, the biologist. Share what's happened.

"I don't think she comes into your yard intentionally," she says. "I think she's passing through. Your property probably crosses her path between something ripe and edible just now and her den. I wouldn't worry."

Of course she wouldn't worry. She lives in Los Angeles, thousands of miles away, so she's not on anybody's dinner path. And the bear, my bear, doesn't have my daughter's scent in her nose. She has mine.

Unfortunately for me, bears have long memories and this bear has sniffed me twice in a single day. I wonder how long the memory will last, and whether she smells friend or foe.

bear etiquette

NUDISTS HAVE BARE etiquette. One doesn't stare. One doesn't
walk too close or brush past another and touch *by accident*. And when
sitting, the conscientious nudist places an old towel or newspaper on
the seat or bench to keep it sanitary for the next user.

I discover this fascinating information in my morning newspaper on what must be an extraordinarily quiet news day. But evidently
some guys in San Francisco frequent various outdoor nude gathering
places and disobey the protocols. Other folks find this offensive. A
mini storm is whirling. Who knew?

Since I don't live in San Francisco and don't frequent nude parks
or beaches, *bare* etiquette isn't an essential part of my daily life. Instead, I wonder about *bear* etiquette, about the protocol when a bear
has come into sight. Perhaps I should call and warn my neighbor at
the cottage, or phone the couple who live across the highway.

My bear wanders in and out of my yard several times this third
summer of watching bears, so I have multiple occasions to consider
what makes the most sense. If the bear heads toward the cottage, I
see no reason to phone the people across the highway. And if I see
no car outside the cottage, then I have no reason to phone an empty
house either.

One sunny afternoon, the bear travels one of her usual routes along the drive toward the cottage and I watch. Think about phoning. Just as I reach to pick up the phone, the bear drifts off into the woods. My hand is still in the air when my neighbor emerges from her garage with her mountain bike, hops on and pedals off. She has missed a head-on confrontation with the bear by half a minute at most. Next time I'll call.

☆

This summer, I have ambitious plans. Our front yard looks mostly *as was* when we bought the house. Huge old Norway Spruces, *Picea abies,* dominate the space. Planted perhaps fifty years earlier as lovely ornamentals, they no longer appear lovely or ornamental. They stretch a hundred and twenty feet into the air, with sagging branches at every level. Some branches sweep the ground, creating barriers for walking, creating routes for ground fungus to travel upward and infect the whole tree. Some branches simply droop, making the trees look like elderly ladies in dusty green velvet ball gowns.

These trees are tired with many dead limbs. They shade the house and lawn and would make a wonderful setting for a horror film—dark and foreboding. We've decided to cut down several close to the house—to open the space for light and air, and to prevent mold and rot on the building itself, to allow the roof and clapboards enough sun to dry well between rains.

I also have ambitious family plans. My parents will come for two weeks, staying a week with me, then exploring nearby towns and villages independently for several days before returning home to Ohio. During their visit my older daughter will come by train from New York to see them.

All these plans fall apart. First, my daughter's husband develops a constriction in an artery in his leg. She calls the day before her visit to cancel—he's in the hospital and needs various procedures. It seems serious enough that I'm the one to train south and spend a couple of days with her as he receives the start of a lengthy series of treatments aimed at saving the leg. To do so, I must leave my parents alone at the house with no car.

Although she has gotten speeding tickets in Ohio for driving her age, eighty-plus, on the superhighway my mother isn't comfortable taking me to the train and managing my large vehicle on the strange and narrow country roads. My father no longer drives at all. So what's the etiquette for leaving visitors at your house without wheels or any sort of mobility? I do the best I can, fill the fridge with food, and assemble phone numbers—taxis and other emergency options.

Things turn more or less stable in New York, so when I return to the country three days later, we resume the planned touring about. The Norman Rockwell Museum is a high point. Chesterwood, the home of Daniel Chester French, famous for sculpting the Lincoln Monument, leaves both parents in a state of reverence. We take a day at the Hancock Shaker Village, and explore a beautifully preserved historical setting, complete with heritage breeds of livestock: cattle, *Bos Taurus*, sheep, *Ovis aries,* pigs, *Sus scrofa domesticus*. But again, plans go awry.

My father's legs bother him. He's felt sore all spring, but walking at the village causes serious discomfort. They decide to cancel their independent travel plans and stay with me for the entire visit. But I'm still stressed from the trip to New York and the worry about my daughter's husband.

What is the etiquette for saying, *I've run out of easy outings? I need some time by myself?*

I try to be gracious and head to the grocery store to restock.

☆

As the visit continues, the tree guy saves us from boring each other silly. He arrives early in the morning and climbs a Norway Spruce. Wearing spikes and a safety belt, he scampers up the large scaly trunk buzzing off branch after branch with his chain saw. His assistant on the ground lines up the discards for the chipper. I pop in and out while he works, and at one point he says, "This big one's coming down in a few minutes if you want to watch."

"Sure. Thanks." I know who else will want to watch. I hurry inside and collect my father. We stand on the front porch, where our guy assures us we'll be safe.

Within about five minutes, he sends his assistant off at right angles with a heavy rope, positioned just so. They secure another rope to a distant trunk. The chain saw growls to life again, and as Dad and I watch, this hundred-and-twenty-foot giant trembles, then drops. The earth shakes. I feel the vibrations up through the bricks, through my heavy rubber soles, right up my legs.

My dad smiles and shakes his head. "Can't believe how he could aim that thing," he says. "It's a big one. Glad I got to see it fall."

Later, after lunch, after the chain saw and chipper have quieted, he's still marveling about seeing the tree come down. "Visiting Daniel Chester French's house and studio, and then watching that tree, just about made my visit," he says. "Only one thing more would make it perfect. I'd like to see this bear you've been telling us about."

"Sorry, Dad. I'm not in charge of the bear."

Not a half hour later, as we sit on the sun porch, that familiar shape appears in the yard, this time from the highway. "Look, Dad, Mom. You wanted to see a bear?" We watch until she goes off about her bear business. My father's smile doesn't quit.

I ponder this two-week spell that has been turned upside down. In New York, a young man has experienced damage to his leg by using it too hard—his condition mostly occurs among runners. With excellent surgeons and careful therapy, he will improve and regain full use of his leg.

Here in the country, an old man has damage to his legs due to age; the joints have grown stiff and unreliable. He will not improve. His mobility will continue to deteriorate. But in spite of that, he's had a perfect visit.

I wish I could discover the etiquette for saying thank you to a bear. Probably not a *bear* hug. Not a *bare* hug either.

☆

The secret of all victory lies in the organization of the non-obvious.

—Marcus Aurelius

☆

the wise man

HOMO ERECTUS DOES not refer to a gay guy with a woodie. Bears and bumblebees don't have a lot in common except that they are both kind of fuzzy and round. These two wonderful facts dance together in my mind because of Carl Nilsson Linnæus, *Carolus Linnæus,* 1707–1778. And yes, he does have a Latin name, bestowed upon him by admirers.

While this sounds wild at first, it wasn't unusual. During the sixteenth and seventeenth centuries, educated and intellectual Europeans took up the custom of renaming themselves in Latin, usually translating their names from their native language into the more formal language of the church and of the classical world. Linnæus' Latin moniker came not from his own choosing, but at a time when he was being honored for his scientific work—specifically the bestowing of Latin names on plants and animals, so it has a sort of wonderful circular logic: as he gave the animals Latin names, others gave him one.

This Swedish botanist, physician, and zoologist is the father of modern taxonomy, the systemized organization of plants and animals into groups; he is also considered one of the fathers of modern ecology. Linnæus' work, published as *Systema Naturae*, rests on an impressive tradition—Aristotle and Plato were also interested in classification.

Linnæus, an academic, spent his life searching out and sorting plants, animals, and minerals according to a revolutionary system of his own devising. Linnaean binomial nomenclature (two-word naming) attempts to classify every living organism on the earth with a unique and meaningful name based on structure or properties. This system of organization is endlessly familiar to, or hated by, high school biology students as follows: *kingdom, phylum, class, order, family, genus, and species* (sub-species may also be named). The *genus* and *species* names, in Latin, make up the official binomial label. Various mnemonic devices exist to help students remember the precise order of the system. My favorite is: *Keep pond clean or frogs get sick.* In the case of the black bear, the classification works like this:

Kingdom:	*Animalia*	(animal)
Phylum:	*Chordata*	(vertebrate)
Class:	*Mammalia*	(mammal)
Order:	*Carnivora*	(meat-eater)
Family:	*Ursidae*	(family of bears)
Genus:	*Ursus*	(bear)
Species:	*U. americanus*	(black bear)

This process generates a binomial name of *Ursus americanus*, or, in the case of my bears, the eastern black bear, the sub-species of *Ursus americanus americanus*. Bumblebees, *Bombus terrestris,* are not even close cousins. They have only one classification in common with bears —that of being animals, and at the phylum level, they diverge into invertebrates while bears have sturdy spines. Roundness and fuzziness obviously isn't enough to declare a family connection.

Early on, minerals were dropped from the taxonomy. More recently, the classification system has been modified, due to Darwinian concepts, such that extinct varieties of animals and plants were given the same genus name as their living descendents. Useful clarity.

Enter *Homo erectus*—upright man, an ancestor of *Homo sapiens,* wise man. The translation is important, however. *Homo* in this case comes from the Latin, meaning man; it does not come from the

Greek *homo*, meaning the same, from which we get homophone, homogenized, homosexual. The names *Homo erectus* and *Homo sapiens* come from Linnæus via believers in evolution.

☆

I'm devising a system of my own. Each time a new plant or animal appears for the first time in this text, I include its Latin name. Thereafter I simply use the common name. At first I didn't understand my reasons for doing this—it just seemed sensible. But after some pondering, I realize that I'm drawn to these names—to their scientific accuracy and their musicality. Writers are lovers of words after all—connoisseurs of sound and meaning transcribed into symbol. And some of the sounds are so delicious: *Puma concolor, Acer palmatum.*

At a deeper level, this naming process probably reflects my own classification—*homo sapiens*, wise (wo)man—as well as my very human need to organize and make sense of the huge and confusing world that surrounds me. Otherwise, I'd struggle to cope with all that chaos. (Organizing really is useful. Witness all those reality TV shows and magazine articles about household organization and chaos and too much stuff.) So I believe that the notion of classification goes back much further than the Greeks. It is probably programmed into our brain circuitry and has been for eons.

Unfortunately, classification can go awry. My parents belong to the Greatest Generation. I'm a Baby Boomer. Our children belong to Generation X. Who knows what they'll call our grandchildren? None of this is the fault of the so named grouping—we didn't ask to be born when we were—it just happened. But marketing geniuses love this stuff. It helps them direct Viagra and portfolio management ads to golf tournaments and technology and fast food ads to audiences of soccer matches. That seems harmless enough at first look.

But it's worth taking that second look. As I was growing up, there were two groups of kids in my high school: the good kids (us) and the hoods (not-us). Interesting that in my vocabulary, my group didn't have a pejorative name while the other folks did. Over time the classification system has exploded: geek, jock, nerd, stoner, emo, goth. Yet as far as I can discover, there is no subspecies *Homo sapiens joccus,* or *Homo sapiens stoneria cannabis.*

These stereotypic names do not sing as does *Marmota monax* or *Bombus terestris,* but at least they reflect some sense of choosing. A kid can decide to be studious or to smoke dope or both. Similarly, political groupings seem mostly chosen as do many occupational classifications if one adjusts for socioeconomic class and education.

More insidious are the names that relate to racial, religious, or ethnic groups, or to those with disabilities. As with the generations, belonging to such categories happened to folks through no fault of their own. And yet we make judgments, valuing some highly and others not at all. And most of these judgments seem to reflect that simple discrimination I used as a teenager—us versus not-us. So maybe, for the wise man, it's time to leave high school behind.

☆

In the plant kingdom, issues of classification and organization are less politically charged, although my botanist daughter often reminds me that weeds are just plants growing where we don't want them to grow. It is, in fact, useful to categorize—*leaves of three, let it be,* a sensible warning for *Toxicodendron radicans,* poison ivy. And surely it's helpful to know that *Solanum lycopersicum,* the tomato, is part of the nightshade family and that while its fruits are edible, good for us with all that lycopene, and widely consumed, leaves and stems can be toxic if consumed in quantity. It also helps to know that *Rheum rhabarbarum* stems make great pies and sauces, but the leaves contain oxalic acid, which can be poisonous. Likewise the leaves of all sorts of cherry trees (Genus: *Prunus),* when wilted, contain cyanide and are highly toxic to horses, *Equus ferus caballus.* In the case of plants, then, the discrimination might better be phrased good-for-us versus not-good-for-us.

☆

Bears and bumblebees must make these distinctions according to some *Ursine* or *Bombus* system of classification. Good to eat versus yuck. Bear or bee versus not-bear, not-bee. Female, therefore potential mate, versus male, therefore potential rival. While I believe that bears and bees, along with many other members of the animal kingdom, must make clear judgments and classify the worlds they inhabit, I sincerely doubt that they do so in Latin. Probably just as well. It would be very upsetting to our human sense of our place in the world, to our sense of ourselves as wise folk at the top of some evolutionary pyramid, if we were to come upon a bear in the woods quoting "et tu Brutus," or a bumblebee buzzing along conjugating "Amo, amas, amat." Nope, way too scary.

Everything in life I share, except of course my teddy bear!
—Unknown

ursa major—ursa minor

WINNIE THE POOH, Little Bear, Corduroy, Paddington, Yogi and BooBoo, Goldilocks and her posse. . . . When I stop to consider, it seems extraordinary that we surround small, vulnerable children with stories and images of large, hulking beasts. And then the Teddy Bears! On the second floor of this house I count thirteen bears:

- five teeny bears, two in shirts, two in fur, one wearing a hand-knitted sweater
- one soft brown bear in a dress
- one mama polar bear hugging one baby polar bear
- one Paddington in blue jacket, red hat
- one honey bear with a wind-up key who plays the Winnie the Pooh theme
- one big brown bear with red plaid ears and matching bow tie
- one bear pillow
- one hot pink velour bear with a matching pink bow (my bear)

Bears large and bears small—thirteen of them.

In late 1902 Morris Michtom created the original Teddy Bear for his business, the Ideal Novelty and Toy Co. Inspired by an event during a hunting trip in November 1902 in Mississippi, a political cartoon appeared in the newspapers. President Theodore Roosevelt had been on a hunting expedition, but had not shot a bear. Companions on the trip chased a bear, hounded it, exhausted it and tied it to a tree. When they showed it to Roosevelt, he refused to shoot such a beleaguered creature. In some versions of the story the bear was a cub, sitting in a tree.

Whether the cartoonist intended to demean the President or not, it had the opposite effect. Michtom sent his first bear to the White House and received permission to produce and market *Teddy's Bears*. They quickly became a fad, and Victorian ladies collected *Roosevelt Bears* and carried them about. At approximately the same time, the German manufacturer Steif began making soft, furry, toy bears for children. These days, when early Steif bears show up on eBay they have big prices attached: $2,500 for an old, much loved bear.

Most children in the United States own at least one teddy bear, albeit not with a price tag of $2,500. Some very fortunate adults have their own bears as well, my mother for example. These grown-ups' bears are large—nearly two feet in height—and they have a heart stitched across the chest. They are not soft, cuddly teddies like the ones my father buys for his grandchildren and then his greats. These bears are sturdy and tough—they need to be, for they are huggy-bears or care-bears.

I first met my mother's huggy-bear in the cardiac unit of the hospital as she prepared to return home after a quadruple bypass. In bypass surgery, clogged arteries near the heart are replaced by healthy arteries from elsewhere in the body, most frequently the leg. In the case of my mother, the surgeon made four such replacements to re-plumb her circulatory system. Bypass surgery is highly invasive. In addition to the trauma associated with exposing the live human heart, and the harvesting of healthy leg arteries, the sternum, the breastbone, must be sawed in half vertically to access the chest.

Enter the huggy-bear. After surgery, the sternum is wired back together, but any movement causes pain, even breathing or speaking. Coughing is an agony and could damage the repairs. So when a post-operative patient needs to cough and clear the lungs (a frequent occurrence), she must hug her bear tightly to her chest, which provides a wall of support to the healing tissue. A thick, dense pillow might also be used, but the bear is designed to be the exact right size to hug. Thank you, Morris Michtom. Thank you, Teddy Roosevelt.

☆

Why the fascination with bears? It seems to pervade all regions where bears are common—mostly in the Northern Hemisphere. Bears appear in the stories and folklore of indigenous peoples in Europe, Asia, and North America, but why? Certainly, if a large and impressive mammal makes occasional appearances in your village, you're bound to pay attention. I admit to paying a lot of attention. I'm rapt whenever one wanders into my line of vision and I can do nothing but watch until it disappears. When a bear appears at a restaurant Dumpster in the next town, while people lunch at adjacent outdoor tables, it makes the local papers.

And bears have aesthetic advantages over other creatures, such as, say, *Alligator mississippiensis*. Bear fur is thick and appears soft—even cuddly—as opposed to the gator's scaly hide. Bears don't generally flash those rows of sharp teeth. And they have cute, small, round ears that somehow soften the overall impression of size and mass.

I think the aspect that most endears these large furry beasts to us is their posture. While bears often walk or run on all four legs, they are comfortable standing upright. They even sit back on their derrieres, much as we do. And so, like many of the great apes, they seem familiar to us—similar to us. A kindred species. Highly anthropomorphic of us to think this way, but a likely explanation nonetheless. That's only part of the story. I believe that bears offer us that odd and enticing mixture of beauty and danger—which equals fascination.

So if, perhaps, we are predisposed to like sightings of bears, it makes perfect sense that we'd see them, even in the sky. The ancient Greeks (Ptolomy for example) noted the constellations of *ursa major* and *ursa minor*. Large bear and small bear. I sight these as the big and little dippers, but where I see ladles, many others see that round bear shape with an especially long tail.

This summer, I see not one, but two distinctly different bears at distinctly different times. My old friend, the mature female, shows herself first, making her stolid and determined passages from road to wetland, or else from creek to woods. But a new personality also appears—a smaller, more slender young bear. Perhaps my size, five feet tall, this bear scampers, lopes, gallivants, skips, frolics. And unlike the big bear, Ursa Major, the little one comes right up to the house—often crossing the patio inches from the back door. So close. I could invite it indoors to play. But I don't. Instead, I check the Massachusetts Division of Fisheries and Wildlife for everything I can discover about my new friends.

The appearance of this second bear, Ursa Minor, solidifies my classification of the large bear. She is clearly female and the newcomer most likely her half-grown offspring. Otherwise, she would not allow it to share her territory.

Bears are good mothers, unlike the snapping turtle, *Chelydra serpentina,* whose one act of motherhood after mating takes only a morning. Mother Snapper emerges from the marsh, prowls for several sunny nesting sites, digs holes in loose soil, lays up to fifty leathery eggs, covers the nests and returns to the water, all before noon. I know this because I've watched it happen: a laborious pushing out of egg after egg on a hot summer morning, her neck bent in a rictus of strain. This ordeal provokes in me a certain maternal surge of sympathy. Still, I have to replant a particular section of my entryway hosta garden every June, once Ms. Snapper has finished. Turtle eggs don't care if a plant grows above them or not. They simply need warmth, kindly provided by the sun.

Bear cubs—usually one, two, or three, but litters of up to six have been reported—arrive at the coldest time of year, during hibernation. They stay with their mothers for approximately eighteen months, nursing for the entire time, although as they grow larger, they also forage with their mothers. Mother bear protects her young, often stashing them in a tree for safety while she seeks food. And while many of the reputed bear-human encounter stories or warnings seem to involve a mother with small cubs nearby, she'd rather hide her cubs in a tree than have to engage in aggressive, protective action.

Female bears mother for a relatively long time in the animal kingdom. They usually don't go back into estrus until they have fully weaned and separated the yearlings from their juvenile dependent state. Even then, a maturing adolescent may stay within the mother's territory for another year. From size and behavior I judge the small bear I've seen to be just such an adolescent—still childlike and goofy.

☆

The plumber comes to install a new sink faucet—the old one, original to the house in 1929, has certainly paid for itself by now. He arrives on a day when the small bear has scampered by. I tell him about my two bears as he returns to his truck, new faucet now flowing perfectly. I share my hunch that one is the growing-up cub of the other.

"Oh yeah. That's how it works," he agrees. "But how does it act, the little bear? Purposeful and sensible? Or silly?"

"Silly," I reply. "Why do you ask?"

"My wife has a theory," he explains. "If a bear is sensible—if it's businesslike and goes about finding food directly—it's a female."

That fits with my observations of the big bear. I've called her female almost from the first sighting. "And if it's silly?"

"It's a guy. Bouncing around, acting loopy. No sense whatsoever. You got a teenaged male. You know, like about eighth or ninth grade." He shrugs and grins at me, and I see signs of a certain remembered mischief in his eye. "My wife, she's pretty smart about this stuff."

I laugh, but I have to agree. My Ursa Major is a mature, sensible Mama Bear. My Ursa Minor is a Boy-Bear.

As I wave and watch the plumber drive off, though, I revise my opinion slightly. Quite often that goofiness lasts longer than eighth or ninth grade.

☆

My sister taught me everything I really need to know, and she was only in sixth grade at the time.

—Linda Sunshine

☆

sister bear

WHEN MY OLDER daughter was three, I picked her up from a mothers' day out program. "Congratulations," said one of the caregivers. "Great news."

That stopped me. "Pardon me, but what news?"

"Your daughter said you were having a baby. So congratulations."

I shook my head. "Sorry. I'm not. She's been wanting to be a big sister for a while now, but we're not there yet."

Later at home, I quizzed the chatty little one.

"I've been asking and asking," she explained. "And you said we could have a new baby."

"I said someday, but it's not someday yet." And someday wouldn't happen for another eighteen months, which made for either impatience on my daughter's part or the world's longest human pregnancy on mine.

Nonetheless, once the promised baby arrived, big sisterhood took over and the older child grew very nurturing and possessive of the infant. This continued for quite some time until the littler one grew big enough to talk and have her own opinions, and a more contentious and normal sibling relationship followed. Years down the road the older daughter would sometimes call the younger one Sister Bear, as in, "Hey, Sister Bear."

☆

I remember this ancient history when I see a series of videos produced by a black bear research organization in Minnesota. There, biologists are making a longitudinal study of a clan of female black bears and their offspring. These bears are tracked using GPS collars, and while they grow accustomed to researchers and cameras, they are truly wild bears, going about their bear business.

One winter, a den cam recorded an unusual happening. A mother bear, Lily, has a yearling daughter, Hope, still nursing, still in the den. The mother gives birth to twin cubs. Lily has given birth to Hope a year earlier, possibly the first live wild bear birth ever recorded. But mother bears usually reproduce every other year, and don't generally ovulate while still nursing and rearing a yearling.

The best theory about why this bear reproduced in such an unusual way comes from reproduction and lactation experts. Bears, like humans and many other mammals, produce the hormone prolactin, which has several functions in the body, including the regulation of lactation and ovulation. The experts believe that the single nursing cub might not have provided her mother with enough suckling to stimulate sufficient prolactin to prevent ovulation. The result—a rare mixed-age den.

The videos capture my attention immediately because they're so unusual and so funny. One of the new cubs, probably no more than ten to twelve inches in length, has climbed to the top of the yearling's head and clings there with ferocity. Poor Hope does her best to dislodge those sharp little claws—she brushes her head against her mother's body, against the side of the den, tries to swipe the cub away with a paw, tries to shake it off, but no matter what she does, the tiny creature stays attached. Later videos show the male baby trying to escape the den and explore the snowy landscape outside. Big sister Hope grabs him and retrieves him. She also shares her mother's attention and her milk with both babies. Mother Bear is well equipped in this capacity, as she has six nipples along her chest. In multiple cub litters, each cub may claim a pair to use regularly, sort of a bear version of one's place at the table.

This yearling bear suddenly reminds me of my own older daughter, sort of a miniature mom to her younger siblings. Once the warm weather arrives, Hope continues to nurture the babies and keeps a watchful eye as they explore the outside world, climb trees, dig for grubs and play. It's as if she's showing them, *here's how to be a bear.*

☆

The universe of sisterhood is not one that I've experienced. When I was about three, my mother gave birth to a baby boy afflicted with spina bifida; he died two weeks after birth and I never saw him. My recollections of that time are patchy—a mix-up in suitcases such that I got my father's clothes and he got mine for a night; a hospital photo of a little cute baby; myself standing on the sidewalk outside a tall yellow brick hospital building and waving up to a window at the top, where a pale hand (my mother's) waved back.

Because of that family loss I've lived my life as an only child, with the odd mix of plusses and minuses that ensue. I grew accustomed to having lots of adult attention but was less skilled with peers than children who had brothers and sisters. Adults seemed kind and safe; kids unpredictable.

I loved school, because there I could a.) please the teachers and b.) play with other children and start to understand how to interact. The peer learning always challenged me and I often got into quarrels and scrapes, so I had to develop some toughness, some interpersonal rhino-skin. At home I was mostly on my own and I seem to remember pestering my mother with complaints of *nothing to do,* and so eventually I turned to my imagination and to books.

At some point in adulthood I encountered the phrase, "the self-sufficiency of the only child." It resonated with me immediately and continues to do so. Because I was so often thrown upon my own resources as a child, I feel comfortable in my own company. While I am an extrovert and love gatherings, I can spend longs spells of solitude and entertain myself much as I did as a child—reading, writing, mucking about outdoors.

And so, perhaps I identify with Mama Bear. While she accomplishes her motherhood tasks with toughness, skill and confidence, she spends significant time alone and seems content. I do wonder how that works out for the cubs, though. While some litters include a single offspring, twins and triplets are common. When the time comes for the young bears to go their own ways, I wonder if the twins and triplets will have difficulty separating, if the onlies will have an advantage.

And what about poor little Hope? Will she miss her younger siblings? Will she miss the fun of herding them and bossing them around? Or will she turn into a spectacular mother because of her unusual chance to be a sister-bear?

I plan to stay tuned.

*If God had wanted us to be concerned for the plight of the
toads, he would have made them cute and furry.*

—Dave Barry

fake fur

UPON DISCOVERING MY preoccupation with bears, a friend offers
a caution. "You're not going to turn into a furry, are you?"

"No, that's not on my life list."

Tuscany, Spain, the south of France, these destinations I'll happily contemplate. But putting on a bear suit and hopping the bus to
downtown Pittsburgh for the annual Anthrocon, the furry convention, doesn't appeal at all. Nor does hanging out with four thousand
people dressed as wolves, *Canis lupus,* squirrels, *Sciuridae,* monkeys,
Primate, or even unicorns, but I can find no scientific name for uni-
corn. These fursuits can cost from $500 to $10,000. Ouch!

The furry fandom is an outgrowth (subspecies?) of sci-fi and
comic book enthusiasts. They became an official group at a sci-fi convention in 1980. Interactions occur online for much of the year and
include gaming and role-playing. Pittsburgh, in addition to being repeatedly selected as Rand-McNally's most livable city, also hosts the
largest Furry convention. Hmmm, wonder if these two facts connect.

And yes, rumors circulate about Furry folk and their kinky sexual practices, also known as yiff, both in person (in plush?) and via
the internet (cybersex). These people are mostly college students and
young adults, so odd behavior is certainly possible. Some of the cos-

tumes are clearly provocative. Other costumes or alter egos are huge and require padding, perhaps even a beast-like sumo suit underneath the fluffy fur. So with people wearing all that gear the *what-goes-where* of sex could get quite complicated. Plus I'm quite happily married. So no thanks.

My fantasies run to watching the sun set along the shoreline, not turning myself into an anthropomorphic version of a mammal and spending four days sweating in the cement ambience of the convention center. So in spite of the fact that Pandas, *Ailuropoda melanoleuca*, (literally meaning black and white cat-foot) are a favorite alter ego of some, the Furry universe with all its varieties is not one that I'll investigate.

☆

Real bears do come in interesting varieties, including the Giant Panda. Mostly pandas have been considered true bears, *Ursidae,* but for a period of time in the late 1800s they were reclassified as belonging to the raccoon (*Procyon*) family. They have since rejoined *Ursus,* ringed eyes and a diet of bamboo notwithstanding.

A Chinese legend holds that pandas began as all-white bears, but changed color as a result of grief. A panda cub had joined a flock of sheep herded by a kind shepherdess and he grew to love her. When a leopard attacked the cub, the shepherdess defended him and the leopard turned and killed her. The young panda ran off but returned for her funeral with the other pandas. They rubbed ashes on their arms to display their grief, and as they cried, the ashes made circles about their eyes; when they rubbed their ears, the ashes marked those as well. The girl's three grieving sisters flung themselves into her grave and then all four rose up into a huge mountain, The Four Sisters Mountain, which protects pandas to this day.

Whether this folktale is true or not, baby pandas don't start out with their distinctive markings. They are born tiny and pink, with thin white fur. The coloration of arms, legs, ears and eyes develops slowly during the first couple of months of life until by four months they resemble their parents, just in miniature.

☆

Koalas, *Phascolarctos cinereus*, those cuddly Australian cuties, are often referred to as bears due to their appearance, but they are not bears; they are marsupials. They also might have bad breath from eating all that *Eucalyptus*. And they might be somewhat intoxicated, if one believes contemporary urban legends. Supposedly, some of the chemicals in those Eucalpytus leaves are pretty potent. With or without koalas, and with or without them being stoned, the list of bears is pretty impressive and includes the following:

> *Ailuropoda* (pandas)
> *Tremarctos* (spectacled bears)
> *Helarctos malayanus* (sun bears)
> *Melursus* (sloth bears)
> *Ursus americanus* (black bears)
> *Ursus* arctos (brown bears)
> *Ursus maritimus* (polar bears)
> *Ursus thibetanus* (Asian black bears)

Worldwide, brown bears are most common, ranging from the forests of Europe into arctic and tundra regions of Russia and on into Alaska and North America. Browns include Eurasian brown bears, Far Eastern brown bears, grizzly bears, Himalayan brown or red bears, and Kodiak bears. Browns and polars are the largest of bears, weighing in at about 1,700 pounds, and they are also the most aggressive. The biggest visible difference between these big bears and the others is that that the browns and the polars have a large hump on their shoulders, just below the neck. It makes them look intimidating.

Because of this hulking appearance, and perhaps because our language for bears comes from northern Europe, I'm guessing that some of the ferocious images of bears in our language and culture are based on the browns, rather than on the less fearsome-looking blacks.

Still, folklore and legend point in a different direction when it comes to the big browns. Many stories from northern Europe include a human woman with a bear husband or suitor. In some of the stories (Beauty and the Beast for example) the bear isn't actually a bear, but a man who has been placed under an enchantment. In some stories, the bear father comes to steal away his offspring. But in all the tales, the woman has a kind heart, great love for the husband, and the power of her love transforms the bear/beast into a man, often a prince.

☆

In terms of size, the Asian sun bear is the smallest, ranging from 100 to 140 pounds, depending on gender. It is also called the honey bear because it either has a particularly strong taste for honey and other sweets, or because it has a long tongue well-adapted to obtaining honey from hives, or both. Nobody knows for sure. Named for the pale semicircular sun-like patch on the upper chest, ironically this bear doesn't see the sun, but rather prowls at night and sleeps up high in tree nests during the daytime. Perhaps because of its reclusive, nocturnal nature, this is one bear about which there is little research, not much hard data, few legends. Nobody knows for sure.

☆

Various black bears are mid-sized. American blacks, my visitors, inhabit the North American continent and have a great presence in Native American and Canadian First People legends as spirit guides and totem animals. And how could they not, for they have great presence—period. Beautiful, majestic creatures.

Spectacled bears are the only bears living in the southern hemisphere; they roam mountainous regions of South America, particularly Venezuela. Named for pale circular fur patterns around the eyes that resemble eyeglasses, these bears have evoked an interesting mix of stories—a cross cultural blending that includes the European notion of woman-stealing with the more indigenous belief that bear travels from the depths to the heights, and thus can intercede for humans. Bears with diverse stories in a region with diverse heritages.

Sloth bears live on the Indian subcontinent, and have thick, rough, shaggy looking fur. Like the sun bears, they are mostly nocturnal and spend much of their time in trees. Their name is a puzzle—perhaps they were named because their arboreal behavior resembles that of real sloths or perhaps it's because they tend to move slowly and shuffle about unless under pressure from a predator. Present day, they have a reputation for fierceness, but that seems to connect to a particular bear who may have been mistreated by humans and then turned and killed repeatedly.

☆

As the varieties of bears differ in size and geographical distribution, so too they face different survival risk factors. Like other large mammals, bears in all their home regions suffer from habitat loss—forests are shrinking due to human impact on the environment. At present, Asian black bears and giant pandas are at greatest risk for extinction. Polar bear populations also suffer from the effects of climate change— global warming and technological interventions, specifically oil drilling and pipeline construction.

Brown bears of various types and American black bears are numerous and widely distributed across their ranges; in the case of my bears, their numbers are increasing. The sun bears, sloth bears, spectacled bears and Asian blacks, while at risk due to habitat shrinkage, also face human poaching and predation for food, folk medicine, and sport hunting, as well as capture to secure animals for performing, fighting, and even as pets. As a species, we humans have a very mixed record of living respectfully with our *Ursidae* neighbors. This too is a story worthy of telling. One might even hope for a happy ending.

Recent observations in the Arctic suggest that global warming has unexpected consequences for bears—that as habitats shrink and change polar bears and grizzlies are now sharing some of the same home ranges. As grizzlies range farther north and polar bears head south with melting ice, they are interbreeding. While the many different types of bears are genetically distinct, a number of hybrids have been intentionally bred at zoos between American black, brown, and polar bears. Now that may be happening in the wild and it places additional survival threat for the already endangered polar bears.

I've discovered, contrary to the old stories, zero physical evidence for bear/human hybrids, however. And I'm pretty sure that if/when those furry couples have children, their infants don't slide down the birth canal in fursuits. That would be itchy.

*Life is life's greatest gift. Guard the life of another creature
as you would your own because it is your own . . .*

—Lloyd Biggle, Jr.

build a bear

SEVERAL YEARS AGO, while my father-in-law lived in a special-care, Alzheimer's facility, he and fellow residents made an excursion to the nearby Build-A-Bear Workshop, Inc. There they made, dressed, and outfitted teddies of their choice to bring home to their rooms. While not as lively and interactive as, say, a therapy dog, a teddy bear can be comforting—a soft and warming touch for people with growing cognitive limitations. Many older adults living in such facilities sleep with their bears, just as small children do.

To build a bear, you begin with an empty bearskin—this looks something like one of those empty socks that lives forever in my laundry hamper. Then you move to the stuffing station where a hose attaches to the bearskin and a blower forces in fiberfill. Like the huggy-bears used by recovering cardiac patients, these bears also have hearts, so before stitching up the bear, you insert a heart—solid red or red-and-white-checked. You can also insert scent (ick) and other bells and whistles—actually an audio setup with barks, growls, meows, or for the more adventurous, a pop tune by the newest 'tween heartthrob (double ick). This costs extra, as does all the clothing and even the shoes. The Build-A-Bear menu is sort of a la carte. The initial entrée isn't too pricy, but after adding all the flourishes, the price can be hefty. After stitching and dressing the last stop in bear construction happens at a computer where you name your bear and generate a birth certificate.

This enterprising business began in 1997 and is currently listed on the New York Stock Exchange—BBW. While the shops are highly commercial and to my eye somewhat cheesy, the organization fosters good corporate citizenship. They participate actively in the philanthropic community, supporting in particular nonprofits that work with children's issues.

The business has grown, with stores in 45 states, D.C. and Puerto Rico; Massachusetts has nine and Pennsylvania has eleven. The business also operates internationally, in fourteen countries from Bahrain and Brazil, to Japan, Scandinavia, and the United Arab Emirates, with a huge presence in the U.K. It has recently developed an internet presence, with free games for children. Now hands-on or electronic workshops make it possible to build not only bears but also dogs, bunnies, cats, Minnie Mouse, even a Hello Kitty. There's a line of wild animals, farm animals, zoo animals—practically a course in zoology of the plush variety. You can even build Kermit the Frog and Miss Piggy. The directions make it all look pretty straightforward. Choose a bear, give it a heart of your choosing, stuff it and dress it.

☆

Mother Nature is anything but straightforward in her construction of creatures, the opposite of Build-a-Bear. She took ages to get it right. From fossil evidence, it becomes clear that today's bears have interesting and diverse ancestors. Remains have been discovered from at least fifteen different prehistoric bears, spread over wide geographies and time lines. Researchers study bone structure; they examine tooth size, shape and wear patterns; and they use DNA evidence and carbon dating to try to understand the lives and characteristics of these ancient, absent creatures.

A cave in southern China yielded the skull of *Ailuropoda microta,* a dwarf panda who lived two million years ago. This and the *Ailurarctos,* (cat bear—eight million years ago) are believed to be the smaller ancestors of today's giant pandas. Closer to home, remains have been found of the oldest known bear genus, *Parictis,* who first appeared in North America 38 million years ago. This tiny bear's fossilized skull measures only seven centimeters long or about the size of my fist—a teddy of a bear. It traveled widely from North America and spread to Eurasia and Africa.

At the other extreme, the short-faced bears, *Arctotherium* and *Arctodus,* native to North and South America, may have been the largest carnivorous land mammals who ever lived. Down on all fours, they stood at six feet, but if rearing up on hind legs they could measure thirteen feet tall and weighed in at more than 2,000 pounds. These bears were taller and leaner than modern-day grizzlies and their remains have been found from Florida and Texas, north to New Jersey and most of Canada. Analysis of the fossils suggests that these huge bears, like modern bears, were omnivores.

☆

Having seen modern bears, I have trouble imagining such a giant. I'm a five-foot woman. I try to visualize—what if one of these bears stood next to me, down on all fours? Sure, they're extinct, but they lived in my part of the world. And at six feet, I'd have to crane my neck to look one in the eye.

This would not be a new situation. As a teenager and young woman, I always seemed to find tall boyfriends and prom dates—six feet, six two, six five. Slow dancing was a challenge—no cheek-to-cheek. But I could usually hear his heart beating pretty loudly. For me? I hoped so. More difficult were lengthy kissing sessions. I often ended an evening with a stiff neck, but I didn't let that stop me. I know this was wicked—to hog the tall boys when there were tall girls out shopping in the same boyfriend markets. But those long, lean, rangy guys always caught my eye. They still do.

So maybe I could have dealt with six feet, but thirteen? That's two-and-a-half times my height. While not as tall as giraffes, *Giraffa camelopardalis,* (16-20 feet) the short-faced bear, when standing upright, would have reached the shoulder of a large, full-grown male elephant, *Elephantidae,* and been just about as massive. And while other giants like giraffes and elephants are plant eaters, most bears are omnivores—meat *and* potatoes. So no slow dancing, unless you want to be dinner.

The nickname, short-faced, comes as they had shorter, less pointed snouts than modern bears. In artists' renderings they look like sweet-faced teddies, but huge, ginormous in my grandsons' linguistic universe. They lived approximately three million years ago and their closest living relatives are the spectacled bears of South America. Extinction occurred eleven to twelve thousand years ago, making some of these giant bears contemporaneous with dire wolves, *Canis dirus,* and sabre tooth tigers, *Smilodon* (not actually tigers at all). But still, yikes! A fearsome environment to imagine.

☆

Giants lived on the other side of the Atlantic as well. *Ursus spelaeus,* or cave bears, ranged from Germany, Hungary, Poland, Russia, south to Spain, Croatia and even northern Iran between five million and ten thousand years ago. Huge collections of cave bear bones have been found in limestone caves throughout low mountainous regions of central, eastern and southern Europe and some of the accumulated bones' origins have been dated over a period of 100,000 years.

Contemporaries of Neanderthals, these bears also appear in cave art, in France and Switzerland, both as drawings and in carefully arranged collections of skulls—all skulls facing in one direction, for example. This has led researchers to suggest possible totemic use of these bears by early hominid groups—perhaps the skulls were objects of worship or included in religious rituals. Certainly bears appear in more recent Native American legend and myth, and also in totem pole art. Even present-day, non-Native Americans carve up tree trunks and create chain-saw bears, probably without any religious significance whatsoever. So maybe those skulls were simply trophies, like the antlered deer heads that preside over some people's mantles. Or else they were whimsical and useful—like the cub-sized footstools available from some outdoorsy furniture sources.

Physically massive, cave bear remains show similarities in size and body structure to modern-day brown bears and have inspired the creation of a series of novels by Jean Auel, including *The Clan of the Cave Bear*. Aside from Auel's work, many people today know little about the giant prehistoric bears on either side of the Atlantic. We know about dinosaurs, *Dinosauria,* and wooly mammoths, *Mammuthus Primigenius*, but not huge bears. Perhaps this is because we want to think of our bears cute and cuddly; we miniaturize so they're less intimidating, so we can romanticize them.

☆

While beautiful to watch, polar bears don't fill my heart with romance. But they too have their ancestors, *Ursus maritimus tyrannus,* which translates as *tyrant sea bear*. And tyrants they may have been; with a large, muscular anatomy similar to both polar and brown bears, they roamed the icy landscapes of northern Europe during the Ice Age. As no plants could survive during glaciation, these bears, like today's polar bears, were most certainly carnivores and probably preyed on the wooly mammoth. Another extinct marine bear, *Koloponus,* whose partial remains were found in Newport, Oregon, seems less related to modern bears than to other marine carnivores, such as the sea otter. Yikes and brrrr. The only consolation to a small human imagining life in such a fierce environment is that we'd have probably frozen to death before one of these great bears ate us for lunch.

☆

Unlike the Teddy bear, whose origins are clearly evident and well documented, real bears seem to have evolved in vastly different locales and at different times in history. In the past, they may have gone extinct as climate changed, as food sources and habitat shrank, or as predation and human hunting increased. For those who admire present-day bears, these factors might be worth considering if we hope to have real bears in the real world for our grandchildren and great-grandchildren to admire. Once a live species has disappeared from the planet, it will not be possible for us humans to build a bear to replace it. Except in plush. And over time, even the memory of bears might fade in our species, as other memories have faded for some of our elders—a sorry subtraction indeed.

☆

Broadly speaking, the short words are the best, and the old words best of all.

—Winston Churchill

☆

bear in mind

WHILE OUTSIDE IN the garden, I have been hissed at by a mother deer, *Odocoileus virginianus,* warning her new fawn to stay away from me. Indoors, I've been sung to by three hundred kindergarten children, *homo sapiens rascalius,* all at one time and in unison—astonishing. I've been dive-bombed by a male hummingbird, *Trochilidae,* proclaiming *his* territory on *my* patio, and also by a flock of great blue heron, *Ardea Herodias,* while kayaking on what I thought was open water but what the birds obviously considered as their breeding ground. They took turns, those heron, launching gracefully from their nest tree one at a time, swooping downward toward us, sharp beak leading, then circling back to the tree where another bird took flight and repeated the warning dance. And yes, we paddled away rather quickly.

I haven't yet engaged in conversations with bears, but they do communicate vocally. Bears moan to warn of potential threats or in fear. They bark during times of excitement or alarm, or to give away their positions. They huff during courtship or when a mother wants to warn cubs of danger. They growl in anger, or to send strong warnings to potential threats, or to proclaim territory, or intimidate. Since most of their vocalizations include some level of warning, it might be smart of us humans to listen, if a bear starts to talk to us. And perhaps, as is often wise when confronted with a bigger critter, human or otherwise, not to talk back.

☆

While we don't often get the opportunity to chat across species barriers, we do use *bear* frequently in our human-to-human discourse. Most often it means to carry or endure. We bear up under heavy loads. We grin and bear (or bare) it. We bear arms, bear children, bear responsibilities, bear down, bear witness, bear the blame. We bear ourselves erectly at times, bear gifts at others, and often find something totally unbearable. My ordinary desk dictionary includes five and a half inches of bear definitions that refer to the human activity of bearing, before it even gets to the two-and-a-half inches dedicated to *Ursus.* The Oxford English Dictionary goes on for all forms of *bear* for nearly fifty pages, beginning in the year 950 with *bero,* which referred not to *Ursus,* but to barley, *Hordeum vulgare.* According to the OED, the actual heavily built, thick furred quadruped shows up fifty years later as *wildan beran.*

Then there are the various odd expressions, such as bear trap. I had vague memories of a ski binding with that name. Sure enough, in the days when skis were still made all of wood, a strange cable and teeth arrangement held the boot in place—a bear trap. Clearly named after the ugly, cruel-looking, open-jawed leg trap that people used to hunt and destroy real bears and other large animals, the binding didn't work that well for skiers. It has been replaced many times over with more sophisticated methods of boot restraint. For which my knees and my ankles are quite grateful.

But the story doesn't stop at ski bindings. These days a bear trap may also mean that Smokeys, State Highway Patrol Officers with those recognizable hats, have set up a speed trap just up the road and are waiting with radar guns for you to zip through. Change the spelling a little, and Bare Traps is a brand of shoes—I have a pair in my closet.

Bear claws, likewise, produces the same confusion of reports. Of course, bear claws are the long, thick, sharp toenails of real bears. Unlike the claws of great cats, bear claws are not retractible—they're always in view. And some people wear them, or cheap plastic imitations, as jewelry. Real claw necklaces on a string or as dangling earrings, ick. It reminds me of the day my grandmother, a skilled hunter, offered me a fresh rabbit foot, one she'd just chopped off a rabbit, *Sylvilagus transitionalis,* she was butchering. "It's for good luck," she explained. Maybe lucky for me, age nine, but definitely not for the bunny.

Bakeries make bear claw pastries—a paw-shaped hunk of sweet, gooey dough with frosting and almonds. Before baking, the dough is notched, leaving the impression of individual toes or claws. If given a choice, I'd surely prefer tangling with the pastry variety than with claws attached to a live bear. I didn't know though, about the *Beren Klauw,* a Dutch snack made of a meatball with fried onion rings on skewers. Supposedly, you dip them in peanut sauce, like a satay.

Bear Bottom is the name of an easy ski trail in the Colorado Rockies. Obviously a pun, but spelled b-e-a-r, this trail doesn't officially refer to an uncovered derriere. Another trail on a nearby ski hill takes that honor. While clearing the land for the trail, the workmen tacked up *Playboy* centerfolds for their amusement or amazement. The trail: Naked Lady. But well-clad young females might also have a bear bottom, if they buy their tights from a well-known clothing store. Each pair sports a teddy on the seat.

Occasionally a black bear in a western state or province will have pale amber fur, a golden bear. I'd love to see one of those in the wild, or even in a preserve. Another variety of golden bear that I have seen is absolutely gorgeous—it's a fourteen carat gold stylized bear developed by a designer also in the west, in (where else?) the lofty ski resort town of Vail, Colorado. This bear comes in necklaces, bracelets, rings, and earrings—which are small—called cubs. Or if you really want to empty the bank account, golden bear jewelry can be purchased in gold with pavé diamonds inset. It might not be so bad to have that sort of bear around the neck or hiding in the jewelry box.

Plants also steal bears' common name: bear grass, *Asparagaceae*, a form of yucca; bear oak, *Quercus berberidifolia*, a scrub oak; bear's-ears, *Primula veris,* cowslips; bear's foot, *Helleborus,* the often poisonous Christmas or Lenten rose; and the previously mentioned barley. Some plants even steal bear names in their Latin nomenclature. *Allium Ursinum,* for example, is also known as bear's garlic. And bear's breech is the popular name of *Acanthus, brankursine*, a spiny green plant common in warm climates. Its leaf design is frequently used in architectural moldings and interior design and was especially popular in the Arts and Crafts era. But why it's attached to the bear is a bit of a mystery.

In the old days, bear could also refer to bed linens—specifically pillowcases (pillow-*bere*) and mosquito netting (mosquito-*baires*). Or a basket (*bearleap*). The enterprising writer can use them all in one sentence. *I think I'll just load up a bearleap with several pillow-beres and mosquito-baires.* Right, that's so clear.

And bearskin. The word calls to mind those old-time photos of naked babies, posed modestly, tummy down, on a thick pelt, complete with head and four paws. I've seen just such a picture of my husband's now-deceased father, in an old, ornate frame. But bearskin can also be the name of a hotel, a lodge, an airline in Ontario, a Grimm Brothers fairy tale, a hiking trail, or most famously, a tall military hat. Worn at various times by soldiers and military bands in Spain, France, Italy, Belgium, Canada, Denmark, the Netherlands, and Sweden, the hats are most conspicuous in Great Britain.

The British Foot Guards version, for example, stands eighteen inches tall, weighs a pound and a half, and is made from an entire skin of a Canadian black bear. The officers' hats are made from the fur of the Canadian brown bear and dyed black, as the brown bear has thicker, fuller fur—show-offs, those officers. British hat makers purchase between fifty and a hundred black bear skins each year, but if properly maintained, the caps last for decades; some caps in use are reportedly more than a hundred years old.

Not surprisingly, animal activists protest the destruction of bears that precedes the creation of these heavy, hot chapeaux. I'd protest the onset of neck aches if I had to wear one. And I worry about all those poor, winsome infants who now must have their naked pictures taken against a scratchy, inferior background of fake fur, instead of a real bearskin. To say nothing about the poor, winsome bear cub somewhere whose mother has been turned into a hat. Sounds like a book title by Oliver Sachs.

The gay, lesbian, bisexual, and transgender universe also includes *bears*—hyper masculine, often older guys with big barrel chests and lots of facial and body hair. They present a direct contrast to the slim, young, metro-sexual look one sees in some urban gay settings. Interestingly, among the LGBT communities, young men with a yearning to become gay bears are often called cubs. Mama Bear might be shocked.

If you talk with the animals they will talk with you and you will know
each other. If you do not talk to them, you will not know them, and
what you do not know, you will fear. What one fears one destroys.

—Chief Dan George

going on a bear hunt

ASSEMBLE SIX WOMEN, born in five different decades. Have them
travel and explore together for two weeks. Add wine . . .

The sky darkens around us as we sit on the sun porch. I am teaching a two-week writing seminar at my home in the mountains, and
the five participating students have just arrived and settled in. We've
enjoyed the first of many elegant meals together and I'm refilling
wine glasses.

"You have your course outlines. I just want to add a few details.
The complete day's schedule will appear on the fridge the night before so you'll know exactly what to expect and how to dress and equip
yourselves. And I want to warn you: you're in bear country. We've
had them in the yard this summer."

Reactions are mixed. Two people seem uneasy.

"I'll just be upstairs, taking a nap when it comes by," one says, a
nervous smile on her face.

"And I'll be away, on my Diet Coke run," her roommate agrees.

"I could see it, or not," says the teacher of young children.

The redhead just shrugs.

"Bears? Really? I've got to see this." Michele, the youngest of our
group, commits herself to an endless bear hunt. *We're going on a bear*
hunt. Are you afraid? I'm not afraid.

Whenever we're out in the woods, she has the camera ready. Hikes out front, quiet and watchful. Kayaks up ahead to scout the banks. At the house, she stays outdoors, writing in her journal at the back corner of our land, on the edge of the wetlands, at the farthest remove from roads, houses, civilization. I watch her and hope she wears layers of deet to keep off the mosquitoes, *Culiseta longiareolata*.

Days pass and we explore the physical and cultural wonders of this small corner of Massachusetts. But no bears show. We're writers studying writers: Melville, Hawthorne, Dickinson, Wharton. We're immersing ourselves in the natural world, climbing, swimming, hiking, boating. Still no bears.

The uneasy ones relax. Assume the bears are just another story. I am a fiction writer, after all—a liar by trade. The neutrals think about other things. Only Michele holds out. She asks the lawn guy if he knows any way to attract a bear.

"Burn honey," he says. "They've got good noses."

No thanks. I'll pass. I'm not interested in calling up all the local *Ursus americanus americanus* for a hot honey feast in my back yard. Bears do have good noses and long memories—if they once find food in a location they keep coming back. I am not interested in operating a bear restaurant.

☆

Baiting was an acceptable form of bear hunting in the old days, when people saw bears as nuisances. But these days, both baiting (luring with food) and hounding (literally, chasing with hounds) are against the law in Massachusetts. Nine states, however, still allow hunters to entrap bears by baiting an area with bear food favorites: Alaska, Idaho, Maine, Michigan, Minnesota, New Hampshire, Utah, Wisconsin, and Wyoming. In these states, kill numbers and percentages go up for baited bears as opposed to tracked bears; the hunter is more likely to find a specimen drawn by the food.

Opinions about hunting in general and about baiting in particular are numerous, diverse and sometimes combative, as with other issues in contemporary life. Some believe that all living creatures are sacred and should never be harmed. These folks do not eat meat or use any animal products, and try to protect animals from harm at many levels. Others see humans as an intrinsic part of nature and assert that we too obey the natural law: eat and be eaten. That as alpha predators and omnivores, as creatures atop the food chain, it is natural for us to seek out and eat many diverse foods.

Baiting too has champions and attackers. *Baiting is unfair, like shooting fish in a barrel. The bear doesn't have a chance. Baiting takes away the sport of hunting, the adventure.* On the other side, where baiting is legal, hunters and naturalists believe that it is a kinder option. *Fewer bears are wounded by missed shots. When a hunter sets up a stand near a bait station, the bears harvested have a quick and relatively painless death, not the slow misery of injury due to a bad shot. Hunting for one's own food is not primarily about sport or adventure, but a sensible way to provide for one's family.*

Whether one believes in baiting or not, bears do indeed love honey—it's not a folktale—so it would surely attract them. They'll reach into a nest in a hollow tree and haul out large chunks of honeycomb with their paws. They'll stuff it into their mouths, ignoring and even ingesting the angry stinging honey bees, *Apis mellifera,* that surround them. If a hive is located too deeply in a tree trunk, a bear will use powerful arms to crack open the trunk and feed. Beekeepers in bear country often must protect their hives with electric fencing to prevent destruction.

Like humans, bears are omnivores, eating both plants and animals, to the tune of twenty to thirty-five pounds per day, depending on overall body size and type of food consumed. Unlike us, however, they eat significantly more plants—as Michael Pollan might advise. About 85% of a bear's diet consists of buds, young shoots, berries, fruits, grasses and nuts. Most of their animal protein comes in the form of insects—bees, yellow jackets, *Dolichovespula*, ants, *Formicidae,* and their larvae. Ouch and yuck, no thank you. If I had only those choices, I'd definitely become a vegetarian.

Bears are the ultimate locavore—they eat what grows nearby, which would again please today's foodies. Their diet includes seasonal variety—what is ripening now. The apples on your tree, for example, whose limbs they may break when they climb to eat. And they have long memories; year after year they will return to the same berry patch, the same hardwood area for nuts, the same wetland garden.

These patterns would help me if I wanted to actually hunt a bear, which I don't. Massachusetts hunting guides suggest tracking bears through known or likely feeding areas before the killing season officially begins. Or checking with farmers whose crops or livestock bears may be stealing. That sounds dangerous. I'd just as soon exercise patience and wait till a bear crosses our yard so I can watch from a safe distance.

Bears are adventitious eaters; while they hunt and graze with intention, they also eat what they happen to find by chance. They don't hesitate from scavenging meat or fish from other predators' kills and will occasionally prey on small mammals—young deer, moose calves, *Alces alces*, in the wild, and sheep, goats, *Capra aegagrus hircus*, pigs, rabbits, calves, turkeys, *Meleagris gallopavo,* and chickens, *Gallus gallus domesticus,* among domestic animals. They've been known to steal deer from human hunters as well as from wolves, coyotes, *Canis latrans*, and mountain lions, *Puma concolor*. But they sneak and steal; they seldom fight with these carnivores for a carcass. Adult males are the most common thieves, perhaps due to their greater size, greater appetites, and to their greater home ranges—which puts them in more frequent contact with these chance sources of food.

This willingness to help themselves to other creatures' food often places bears in direct contact with humans. They're drawn by scent to our garbage cans and Dumpsters. In the past, dump bears often clustered in state and national parks, feeding on people-food, until the development of bear-proof dumpsters with strongly latched lids and until parks published clear instructions for campers to clean up outdoor grills and not store food in their cars. Even now, with better technology for protecting garbage, human food appeals to bears.

And when they come close enough to steal our food or trash, when they approach these *artificial food sources,* some believe that they may lose their natural shyness toward people—there goes the safe distance notion.

If you live in bear country as I do, and leave a pizza box or Chinese take-out packages on a sun porch, you can almost guarantee a torn screen and an uninvited visitor. Put out birdseed before hibernation, and you'll find the feeder batted down, smashed and emptied. Store pet food in your garage and it won't be your car that gets stolen. It seems a bit like when I walk past the McDonalds, sniff, and note a sudden craving for salt and grease. I too, sometimes find myself an adventitious eater.

☆

It's late in the afternoon, near the end of the student trip. We've been paddling kayaks in the river with a muddy takeout. People go their various ways—some to get clean, some to clean the boats. Michele, our intrepid bear hunter, has stripped down to her bikini and I itch just watching her stride confidently toward the wetlands yet again. Mosquito heaven.

When the bear comes by, the napper is indeed napping. The Diet Coke junkie has borrowed a car to resupply her habit in town. The redhead and I are out of sight, scrubbing river mud off the boats down in the driveway. Michele sits out at the edge of the wetlands fighting off mosquitoes and writing in her journal.

Only the teacher of young children sees him, the youngish bear. He skips across the patio like one of her kindergarteners might, right by the back door to the sun porch. "I wanted to open the door and call out to Michele," she explains. "But I thought if I opened the door, he might be foolish enough to come in."

And yes, if he is a young boy-bear, indeed he might just be foolish enough to come in. Just as our youngest girl-student has been foolish enough to stay out.

If an animal does something, we call it instinct; if we do the same thing for the same reason, we call it intelligence.

—Will Cuppy

small ears

I AM HARD at work, stripping ugly blue checked wallpaper from the third floor guest room. I've decorated the space in red toile and cream, so the blue checks have needed to disappear for a long time. Under the paper, I discover a pleasing surprise—a soft, dusty rose paint. Drab on its own, it will sing with a simple over-sponging of white. Much easier on the painter—me—than the usual primer plus two finish coats.

From the open window, I hear the roar of the mower—the lawn guy. I leave the walls to dry and hurry down to say hello. I value company in the country and have been conversing with walls for two days.

"Oh, you're here after all," he says.

"What do you mean?"

"I knocked, but nobody answered."

I explain about the third floor project. "What's up?"

"A bear came by. Thought you'd like to see."

Rats, I've missed it. "Really? How big?"

"Not too big—one-sixty-five maybe. Just a little guy."

Not too big for him, but plenty big for me. "How do you decide if it's big or just a little guy?"

"It's all in the ears. Check out the ears and if they look big, you've got a small bear. But if the ears look small—watch out, it's a big guy."

"Thanks. Good to know." I seriously doubt that the next time I see a bear close-up, I'll have the presence of mind to check out the ears.

I'm guessing my friend has seen the smaller of my two bears—the one I think of as Ursa Minor. But as the summer progresses, the juvenile will eat well and grow to nearly full size. If it is, as I've speculated, a Boy-Bear, this will be his last summer nearby. The real *big guy* —one of the mature males who mated with the mother—claims a territory of approximately 120 square miles and will drive all younger males away. If the young bear is female, her mother will occupy a range of 9-10 square miles and refuse to share territory even with a daughter bear. She may chase the younger bear away and force her to find her own space, but it may be nearby or adjacent to the mother's.

Except when mating or when rearing young, bears live solitary lives. For most of the year, males spend their days alone. Females give birth every two years on average, so the summer after they wean one brood, they may get a season off the mommy track.

During mating season, between mid-June and mid-July in Massachusetts, these patterns change dramatically. When a female enters estrus, she travels miles, considerably beyond her usual territory, marking the ground with her scent. In the process she may enter the territory of more than one mature male. It could be that the bear I've been watching is not actually crossing between food source and home. Instead, she could be casting about for mates, looking for a party in my yard.

☆

At thirteen, I became fascinated by the notion that at some point in time there might be two boys who liked me at the same time—to the point that they'd actually engage in a fistfight to prove their affection. For a skinny, gawky girl with braces on her teeth and no boyfriends at all, this image seemed most romantic.

The one and only time such a fight took place, I was sixteen and on a group trip during winter to a snowy farm in Upstate New York. We'd been out at night, ice skating then playing in the snow. When we went inside, these two boys, seeming without warning or provocation, started slugging each other.

I had no clue what was going on as their respective friends pulled them apart. Then somebody told me: they were fighting over me. It took me a minute to process that information. Sure, it was possible. I liked both of them, a bit, and had flirted with both, a bit. But nothing serious, at least not to me. The fight was serious though, and it embarrassed and appalled me. Nobody got hurt, but I immediately dropped my crushes on both boys and transferred my flighty teen-aged affections to another boy nearby.

For bears, the situation would have happened differently. While two males in the vicinity of a female in heat will wrestle to prove dominance and chase off a rival, they do not usually fight to the death. (My boys didn't do that either, thank goodness.) They may bite or claw one another, and some large older bears carry scars about their faces and necks from such fighting. But the bear who drops back may simply bide his time. He may get another chance with the lady bear of his choice.

As in some human societies, both genders take multiple partners —a male's territory may encompass the ranges of ten to fifteen females, many of which may be in estrus during the early summer. Should these philanderers perhaps be called *Playbears?* Whatever we call these males, they work hard at their reproductive duties—and lose significant weight during mating season as they do during hibernation. Too busy to eat?

Females with young cubs will be ignored during mating season— they are out of estrus. But as mentioned earlier, available females may cross multiple territories and attract more than one male. They will mate sequentially during estrus, a few days with this partner, a few days with that one, which may result in a litter with mixed paternity. And the females do forage during mating season, so do not lose weight like the males do.

Preliminary courtship can take days—chasing, sniffing, playing, generally getting to know each other. Mating, also, is not a one night

stand—a pair will mate repeatedly over a period of days and the dura-
tion of copulation will stretch from a few minutes at first contact to
a full hour later on, reportedly an amazing sight to see. I'm not sure
I really want to watch, though. In the human community public dis-
plays of affection make me turn away, or want to shout "get a room."

An hour seems like an extremely long time to stay hooked up,
but it makes some sense, particularly from the male bear's point of
view. An hour-long period of intromission (the time while the male
is inside the female) might enhance his standings in the sperm com-
petition, such that if a female has multiple matings, he wants to up
the chances of his sperm reaching and fertilizing an available egg, thus
carrying his genetic material into the next generation. Then too, the
male bear is not without erectile enhancements—no bear Viagra or
Cialis but he has a *baculum,* also known as a penis bone, penile bone
or *os penis.* Humans are one of the few species missing such an interesting anatomical feature.

Most mammals have such a bone that aids in maintaining a long
sexual engagement: primates; most rodents (but not rabbits, and they
seem to do fine without one); dogs; cats, large and small; even bats.
The theory goes something like this—in animals with a relatively
short, obvious, and infrequent period of estrus, a prolonged sexual
contact is more likely to result in pregnancy. In creatures such as
ourselves (and maybe those bunnies) ovulation occurs frequently and
is not as obvious, so shorter and more frequent sexual contact is
needed to reproduce. Regardless of the explanation, all this physiology does shed potential new meaning on the old term, "boner."

When I mention all this to some friends, one guy suggests I do
more research—he wonders if the *baculum* might be used in some
obscure alternative medicines to power up male human sexuality. I
search as he suggests and find quite different results: *baculi* from
coyotes, raccoons, badgers, *Mustelidae,* have all been fashioned into
key chains and are available for sale on the internet for about ten
dollars each. An interesting way to manage the opening and closing
of doors.

I also discover an amazing speculation about why human males are missing the *os penis*—that when the deity created Eve from Adam's body, it wasn't a rib that was removed, but the penis bone. I'm not sure how to react to that. As bones go, the *baculum* is rather puny.

I've seen internet photos and videos of bears mating, and then of course, I wonder who took those photos. Even with telephoto lenses, it seems amazing that the photographers got so close. Obviously bears are not particularly protective or private at such intimate moments and they have no concern whatsoever about exhibitionism or voyeurism. Or maybe all that thick fur keeps privates private.

Once the cycle has finished, sows have been reported to be short-tempered—grouchy as a bear? While they spurn further contact at that time, they do mate repeatedly with some of the same partners in subsequent seasons. As in that movie, *Same Time Next Year?*

☆

Like many creatures in the wild, bears' reproductive cycles and the likelihood of successful breeding depend on the food supply. A heavy, healthy female will be more likely to bear live young and nurse them into full growth than a younger, smaller sow. Larger, older females often bear twins or triplets, while a young bear might birth only one cub.

After a summer with a plentiful food supply, a female will be more likely to bear multiple cubs; after a drought year, the same bear might bear one or none. Similarly, if the food supply is sufficient, the survival rate for cubs goes up, while drought years increase cub mortality percentages. Most challenging for the bears are the years in which this alternates—if three cubs are born after a lush summer and emerge into a meager feeding season two negative factors work simultaneously: less food and more hungry bears. Therefore fewer cubs survive. Over time it evens out, but Mother Bear is particularly well-equipped to respond to such season-to-season variations.

After breeding in early summer, her tiny ball-shaped embryo floats free in the uterus for several months. It implants in the uterine wall in November, just before hibernation, but only if the female is well-nourished. Such delayed implantation helps to guarantee that a healthy mother will produce healthy cubs. A Skinny-Minnie of a bear won't actually get pregnant. In a similar way, a large, strong, dominant, alpha male will be more likely to mate successfully with several fertile females than a young, little guy.

Strange echoes bounce in my mind when I compare this behavior with what I know about human reproductive patterns. At various times and places in our history we've operated under somewhat similar constraints. A male has had to prove himself strong and powerful—by building a home, a herd, a farm, a bank account—before he can win a mate. And sometimes those alpha male humans—politicians, sports and movie stars—engage with many women. Tabloids anyone?

But the notion of a strong, mature, powerful female as a sex object seems a bit less familiar unless one travels to Cougar Country. Instead, in our contemporary society we glorify the childlike waif of a supermodel who may be intentionally so poorly nourished that she has compromised her own reproductive capacity and inhibited ovulation. This same phenomenon actually happens to female bears when food grows scarce and they lose significant body weight—they go out of estrus. And teen or adolescent pregnancies tend to be more high-risk, in people as well as in *ursa*.

For bears, then, large equals mature equals healthy equals reproductively successful. Look for those small ears and you've got a sexy female bear. If only life were that simple in people—if only we females could be large and mature and irresistible.

Only mothers can think of the future—because they give
birth to it in their children . . .

—Maxim Gorky

☆

babes in the woods

BEARS DON'T HOP. Kangaroos (*Macropus*) don't climb trees.

At first look, black bears and kangaroos don't have much in common, except in the world of A.A. Milne. In real life, they live on different continents, in different hemispheres. Bear's winter is kangaroo's summer and vice versa. Bears live solitary lives, while kangaroos live in herds or groups called mobs.

Despite enormous differences, bears and kangaroos share one odd physiological trait—they give birth to tiny offspring in relation to overall body size. Kangaroos give birth approximately one month after conception; the joey is about the size of a bumblebee or a lima bean ($1/30$th of an ounce). It crawls from the birth canal up into the pouch and climbs inside where it will nurse and continue to grow. It will remain in the pouch for about nine months.

Bears give birth eight months after conception, but only three to four months after the embryo actually implants in the uterine wall and starts to develop. Cubs arrive in the middle of the North American winter, while the mother is denned up in hibernation. Mothers deliver one to three cubs and nurse them for several weeks in the den, protecting them from the cold by blocking the den's opening with their backs. A newborn cub looks like a tiny grey puppy. It measures eight inches and weighs eleven ounces, about the size of my hand, from wrist to fingertip.

☆

As a woman with two pregnancies, two children, I'm jealous of these easy deliveries. Popping out eleven ounces—really! As opposed to seven and a half pounds. Mama Bear is twice my size. But then I didn't actually pop out either of my children. I couldn't stretch, so both my daughters were extracted via cesarean section with the resultant miserable, sore, cut muscles afterwards. I doubt they do that with bears. And Kangaroo—from what I've discovered it seems like the joey does all the work, not exactly a lot of maternal labor involved. Totally unfair. (I refuse to even imagine the case of the black rhino, *Diceros bicornis,* at the local zoo, who, after fifteen months of pregnancy just gave birth, in fifty minutes, to a daughter who weighed seventy pounds—ouch!)

For comparison, an average ten-pound house cat bears a six-ounce helpless kitten, weighing half the size of a baby bear. That seems amazing when I think about their relative adult sizes. Likewise, a newborn mouse is similar in size to a joey, (and they're both pink, hairless and ugly) yet the relative sizes of mature mouse and kangaroo are enormously different.

Bear cubs will increase to three hundred times their birth weight as they mature. Humans grow to twenty-two times birth weight and kittens to twenty-five times, so we're more like cats. Not something I was expecting. For kangaroos, I can't even begin to do the math.

If human newborns were as proportionally small as bear cubs, they would weigh in at slightly less than half a pound. There are no recorded surviving human infants with such low birth weights and yet tiny bear cubs routinely survive and thrive. To say nothing of those bumblebee-sized kangaroo joeys. How can such minute offspring reach adulthood?

Kangaroo's pouch acts as an external womb, offering warmth and protection. Once the joey attaches to a teat, it will stay attached and feed for months. Mother Bear dens up with her well-furred and insulated back acting as a thermal barrier against winter's chill which protects her own vulnerable nose as well as her small babies. Each cub selects a particular nipple or pair of nipples and nurses frequently. Even though her body is in hibernation mode, Mother Bear rouses enough to care for her babies and to protect them from freezing in the spring snowmelts.

We humans have a longish gestational period—ask any woman in her eighth month of pregnancy—and an extremely long infancy and childhood period—ask the parents of adolescents. We don't have pouches, but in many cultures around the globe, mothers tie infants in slings across their midsections, about where kangaroo's pouch is located. Some of us strap our babies onto our backs in positions similar to primates or opossums, *Didelphimorphia*. And while we don't den up, or have fat, thickly furred backs (except for some guys who aren't likely candidates for pregnancy or childbirth anyway) we do construct shelters, for ourselves and our families, to protect from extremes of heat and cold.

☆

Every time I walk outside, one of the two robins, *Turdus migratorius,* nesting in the magnolia tree, *Magnolioideae,* next to my kitchen door propels itself out from the thick, shiny leaves to perch on a high branch of the pin oak and scold. When I have ventured to what the bird must consider a safe distance, it arrows back to resume nest-sitting, or later in June, to continue hauling worms to the greedy chicks. The same thing happens when I approach my back door from the yard—escape and return. It must be exhausting for the poor birds, but I can't help thinking this is a dumb place to build a nest. The same pair of robins returns to this tree year after year, however, so they obviously don't care about my opinions. They probably believe this is a dumb place to build a door.

Intentionality is quirky. I've never stashed a newborn, child or grandchild in a white pine like bear does, but I have used a playpen/pack and play. I can personally swear to the presence of non-intentional, nest-building instincts as well. Why else would a woman who couldn't even see her own toes climb a six-foot ladder and roll yellow paint onto nursery walls? (All the while being scolded for her foolishness by her husband.) Or clean and scour the entire kitchen a week before delivery? Bake endless batches of cookies even though her stomach has little room for food with all that kicking baby in the way? I have done all these things, guilty as charged. But those aren't the worst. In our family we joke that our second daughter was fertilized twice—once in the usual way, and then again when I was hauling a wheelbarrow full of horse manure uphill and it dumped all over me, eight months along. I wasn't just prepping the house for the baby, I had to cultivate and tidy the garden too.

☆

And then there's the matter of names. Almost from the first moment I discovered I was pregnant I pondered naming my children. Who were they and how should they be addressed? We didn't know genders ahead of time so selected boy and girl names, though the boy names went unused.

I wonder about animals. Do they *know* they are pregnant? Do they nest instinctively or intentionally or some of each, as we seem to? Do they name their offspring? Kangaroo's baby is always called a joey, but that's a small-case *j*. Who knows about a particular roo—he might be Harry or Aiden.

Can a mother bear with three cubs count? Can she distinguish between her babies, prodding the slow one along, *come on, Matthew, you can do it,* or swatting the one who rushes ahead and puts herself at risk, *get back here right now, Sassy.*

I dig for more information and find research that suggests that many animals can make sensory and perceptual representations— that they can reliably perceive shape or color. They can also remember things, for they return again and again to a place they once discovered food. They shy away from enemies. And they have some sort of core numerical cognition—they can perceive and respond to more versus less.

Psychologists consider responses to number a sign of higher intellectual development, and so they have studied such responses in pre-literate infants, non-counting human populations, primates, dolphins, birds and fish. In spite of Pooh being a bear of little brain, real bears have large brains, relative to overall body size (sorry, Mr. Milne). They've been studied recently as well, by Jennifer Vonk of Oakland University and Michael J. Beran of Georgia State. In simplest language, the researchers trained bear cubs to respond by pressing a nose to an image on a computer screen. When given two arrays of colored dots, one young, captive bear was trained to respond to the larger quantity and given food rewards when successful. Two other cubs were similarly trained to respond to the smaller quantity. While choosing the larger array seems intuitively sensible—more food, more food—selecting the smaller array does not. As with other tested populations, both human and animal, the cubs were more able to distinguish between few and many when the differences were dramatic.

Research also seems to point to three as a sort of magic number—that tested populations can understand three quite reliably, while after three they tended to approximate. Three cookies on the plate seem more desirable to various experimental subjects, human and animal, than two, for example. But at four or more, things get a bit muddled and subjects seem to display a more generalized sense of *lots*.

I wonder why that is and if it's physiological in origin. We humans (and bears) have two eyes, two ears, two nostrils, two arms (forelegs), two legs (hind legs). Perhaps three is a noticeable anomaly. At one time, I lived next door to a family with triplet boys, and it struck me how much more difficult three infants were than two. With twins, a mother can carry a baby in each arm. Triplets require an extra set of hands. It's a whole other dimension. If Mama Bear does indeed have triplet cubs, she probably can count to three and keep track pretty well. Fortunately, her cubs are mobile early in life, so she doesn't have to carry them about. If she has more than three babies, it might get a little more difficult, not unlike the situation in human families.

So translation? I'm a little like Kanga and a little like Bear. I can hop and I can climb trees. And Bear—she just may be able to do the math.

lions and tigers and bears . . .

IN EARLIEST USAGE, cub appeared as cubbe, but by Shakespeare's time (*Twelfth Night: O thou dissembling Cub . . .*) more modern spelling prevailed. In addition to being a noun, which refers to the offspring of various animals, cub can also be a verb, meaning to bring forth cubs, as Mama Bear does, or to live as a cub, as Baby Bear does. But it can also mean to be cooped up, cubbed-up. Which may be where we got the name for cubbies, those little square bins, beloved of preschoolers, where they stow their many treasures. Which might just include a Teddy bear, or at least a cub.

☆

Lions, *Panthera leo*, and tigers, *Panthera tigris,* and bears all have cubs. So do cheetahs, cougars, wolves, leopards and pandas (*Acinonyx jubatus, Puma concolor, Canis lupus, Panthera pardus, Ailuropoda melanoleuca*— what a mouthful). Add badgers, bobcats, coyotes, foxes, hyenas, jaguars, llamas, raccoons, and walruses (*Mustelidae, Lynx rufus, Canis latrans, Vulpes vulpes, Hyaenidae, Panthera onca, Lama glama, Procyon, Odobenus rosmarus*—whew!). According to some lists even sharks, *Selachimorpha,* have cubs. Oh my!

Calves are fairly popular too. They show up in the broods of cows and oxen and elephants, even whales, *Cetacea*. Most oddly, glaciers are said to calve—this happens when a huge chunk of ice drops off the main body of the glacier. Unfortunately, this is happening frequently these days. Global warming anyone?

Kit or kittens arrive with great regularity, as offspring of everything from cats and chinchillas to weasels and woodchucks (*Felis catus, Chinchillidae, Mustelidae, Marmota monax*). Meanwhile, pups are born to armadillos, bats, beavers, mice, rats, and sea lions *(Dasypodidae, Chiroptera, Castor Canadensis, Peromyscus, Rattus, pinnipedia)*. Various horse-like animals give birth to foals, and deer in many regions have fawns.

Most chicks are feathered friends, offspring of various birds, but some waterfowl babies have unusual names—swans, *Cygnus,* hatch cygnets or flappers, geese, *Anserini,* have goslings, and ducks, *Anatidae,* have ducklings. And it's sometimes hard to reconcile the notion of chick—as in soft, fluffy Easter chick—to the reality of, say, the eagle chick, *Haliaeetus leucocephalus,* I saw in a nest in the Pacific Northwest with its huge head, bulging eyes, and sharp beak, who can down an entire salmon, *Salmonidae,* in one gulp. The ultimate anti-cute baby.

An unwise name for offspring applies to many fish, who in tiny versions are called fry. Tempting us to get out the skillet and cornmeal. But you can't blame the mother and father fish. We humans invented those names, they didn't. Plus a fry isn't exactly a mouthful, to eat or to speak, so most likely if caught it will be released.

Then there are the true oddballs. In *Winnie the Pooh,* Kanga has a baby called Roo, but in real life the Aussies call that baby and the koala's a joey. But then these are the same folks who call young women sheilas. Maybe it comes from living upside-down on this earth.

Milne did get Piglet right, but where in the world did tadpoles and pollywogs come from (other than mama frogs or toads, both *Anura*)? It's a mystery. As is the cria, offspring of alpaca, *Vicugna pacos.* Infant oysters, *Ostreidae,* are called spat, most insects, *insecta,* hatch larva or nymphs, and pigeon babies, *Columbidae,* are called squabs or squeakers while partridges, *Phasianidae,* have cheepers. Perhaps best of all is the platypus, *Ornithorhynchus anatinus,* whose little one is a puggle—those Aussies again. Sort of makes one want to snuggle.

Primates of all sorts have infants, as we do. But only people and goats have kids. And when I visit the goat farm and watch small ones at play—butting into each other, climbing to the top of whatever structure is nearby, nosing into anything out of the ordinary, like my pockets, they do remind me of human toddlers.

☆

Back to cubs. I wonder why so many of the cubs belong to animals that seem threatening or ferocious when grown, while calves are mostly horned, leggy grazers, what the circus folk call *hay burners.* Pups and kits are, on average, smaller than cubs or calves, and in many cases they're cute. So it seems mysterious that we have Cub Scouts instead of Pup Scouts, for example. In my experience eight-year-old boys are generally cute and funny, missing a tooth or two and telling endless knock-knock jokes. They do sleep in pup tents, and they don't generally snarl or extend their claws (unless they stayed up all night in those tents).

And what in the world are WEBELOS? A longstanding connection exists between scouting and the military. Retired soldiers often serve as scoutmasters, and serious scouts often join the armed forces when they grow up. Both groups use acronyms. WEBELOS are a good example. In the early days, the youngest boy scouts were called Wolf Scouts. Somewhat later the name changed to Cub Scouts. In its earliest incarnation, WEBELO was an invented word using the first letters of three totemic animals in the scouting world: wolf, bear, lion. As time passed the organization seems to have invented a new meaning for the pseudo-word. In the reverse of the usual process—take some words and turn them into an acronym—someone took an acronym and found a new phrase for it, in this case, *we'll be loyal scouts.* Odd and odder.

☆

Of course the reporting of all this might be somewhat suspect, as I'm no scouting expert. In fact, I flunked out of Girl Scouts, twice. Once as a Brownie and again as a real Scout. I think it was mostly the uniforms that caught my attention—we could wear them to school on scout meeting days. They had those funky scarves. But the meetings bored me.

Early on in Brownies, they gave us strips of paper and precise instructions about how to weave them into a sort of placemat for the butt, known as a *sit-upon*. No skipping strips, no crooked weaving. Once we completed this task, we sat upon our *sit-upons* and proceeded to stitch a badge onto some part of the uniform. Stitching for a seven-year-old meant poking a sharp needle into some cloth, poking a sharp needle into a finger, bleeding all over the badge, getting the thread tangled, crying in frustration. So I quit.

I quit Girl Scouts too, after we bought the uniform, once I realized that they expected us to go on overnight campouts in the woods. I wasn't very good at in-the-house sleepovers. Fine if a friend came to my house, but stay in somebody else's house all night? No way. I missed my mom and dad. I usually ended up calling home at about eleven p.m. with a teary plea, *please come get me.*

As an adult, however, I have learned all these various skills and more—I'm a knitter and quilter, like to make and build all sorts of things, and love to travel. While I enjoy my home, I'm always ready to explore a new state, or country, or continent. I've also slept out in the woods at night, in tents and under tarps and in teepees—and enjoyed it. So maybe I was just a late bloomer. Or maybe I prefer to learn things on my own.

Another possible reason for flunking Girl Scouts might have been the girl factor. In every town and neighborhood of my childhood, I was surrounded by boys of my age, not girls. I raced with boys, climbed trees, explored the woods, built forts, fought in mock battles, played baseball. I never quite mastered the more girly pursuits, nor did I understand the allure of jacks, clapping games, jumping rope. In school, as well as in the neighborhood, I preferred boys as playmates. So maybe I'd have done better in the Boy Scouts. They got to be Cubs, rambunctious little critters, while we got to be Brownies, either a.) a sweet chocolate dessert or b.) a made-up elf creature. Then as now, however, cross-dressing was definitely a scouting no-no.

Animals are reliable, many full of love, true in their
affections, predictable in their actions, grateful and loyal.
Difficult standards for people to live up to.

—Alfred A. Montapert

dancing bears

SWANS MATE FOR life, or so the folklore goes. People who study swan DNA, however, suggest that perhaps extracurricular sex and even divorce occur in this species. I'm relieved to discover this, somehow. As a child of a loving, long-lasting marriage, sixty-plus years and counting, I've always felt a failure for having a marriage end in divorce. If swans really were as monogamous as the old stories would have us believe, that would make me feel terrible. I've behaved worse than some small-brained, ill-tempered bird. Not as bad as the bears, who have those on-again, off-again relationships, but still. As a kid, I got As in every subject except handwriting (grade 3) and physics (grade 11). But somehow I failed at one of adult life's most significant tasks.

Nothing like a family wedding to bring all these old conflicts back to the surface.

My first husband and I began the unraveling of our family when our daughters were five and one. At the time my mind darted from one grim worry to another. Fears about reaching a custody arrangement, finances, selling our house and rebuilding a home on my own consumed me. But right there, center stage in my mind, was the absolute conviction that by getting a divorce, we were somehow wrecking every possible future moment of celebration that might occur at any time in our daughters' lives.

Graduations, preschool through college, they were all the same, all forever tarnished. The very worst, of course, were their weddings. I'd close my eyes and imagine these lovely young women wearing long white dresses and marching up the aisle while their father and I wept and raged and generally misbehaved. It didn't occur to me at the time that I might use my mental energy more profitably to figure out how to cope with the coming days or week—to get myself to the grocery store and manage bedtime. No, I had to imagine every possible disaster that might occur twenty years in the future; I had to say goodbye to a future I'd always taken for granted.

In fact, my older daughter had a beautiful wedding a few years ago. She asked both her father and her stepfather to escort her down the aisle and it was a joyful moment. Everyone behaved. Everyone got along. I found it especially shocking when my ex-husband and his wife laughed at my jokes—as if we were old friends or something.

I sat next to my two-year-old granddaughter (first child of my stepson) and she happily announced the bridesmaids: "Look. Aren't they beautiful?" And then the bride: "Look, Grandpa is bringing her to the wedding!" How could anyone be the slightest bit sad with a small, chirpy child doing the voice-over?

That older daughter is now expecting her first child and will be one of her sister's attendants. She's been advised to hold her bouquet atop her large belly to make it less noticeable. Their half sister will be the other attendant, which seems exactly as it should be. This younger daughter, the soon-to-be-bride, is less traditional than her sister, has asked me to escort her. And by the way, her sisters will be wearing white sundresses. She's chosen royal purple. And her stepmother will make her dress.

☆

"Where's the leach field? Where's the tank?" I ask.

"Don't worry. I'll find them." A man stands with a small sledge-hammer and a metal stake, studying the plot plan for our property, specifically, the septic system. He hammers the stake into the ground at various locations and then pulls it up.

This technology puzzles me. For most of my life I've understood the functioning of flush toilets and municipal sewer systems. Waste goes in and I send it away. Some miles of huge-diameter pipe later, the sewage gets filtered, aerated, treated, and the cleaned water returns to the landscape.

But here in the country, I have no idea. And we need to locate what's under the ground before other men pound in huge metal stakes to support a big tent for the wedding. It will not be helpful if the septic tank suffers a puncture three days before a hundred people gather on our lawn. I'd like our guests to remember the beautiful bride, not the smelly tent. I wonder about ordering a couple of porta-potties. Supposedly they now rent *luxury* versions, quite an oxymoron.

I also wonder about the whole outdoor wedding scenario. I love the wilds, but a wedding is a civilized undertaking. I'm not sure that wild is really better than tame. My daughter is a botanist—she wants to say her vows under the open sky. But she lives in Southern California and there the sky is less clouded, the climate dry.

"What about thunder and lightning?" I ask my husband on the phone as I sit and stare out at a big evening storm in mid-June. "Those metal tent poles, they're great conductors of electricity. If we get a booming light show of a storm, what then?"

"I don't know. It's probably too late to book a back-up."

I ponder the house, a center hall colonial. "How about this? The bride and groom can stand in the front entry with their attendants. Our families can sit in the living room, the groom's in the dining room, and all the kids and young friends will squeeze in; they can pack the stairs."

"You think we'll all fit?" I hear skepticism in his voice.

"Sure. And then the caterers can set up food stations all over the first floor and no one will go hungry, or get fried by lightning." It's the best I can do.

"You're making a big deal. We'll just hope for a sunny day," he says. Then again, he's not sitting on a sun porch surrounded on three sides by a boom and flash downpour. And he's never been, nor will he ever be, the mother of the bride. Worry is part of the job description.

Soon after, his brother calls. "Do you have any back-up plans for bad weather?" he asks.

He's not reading my mind. His call makes perfect sense, as my brother-in-law lives in Boston and has been putting up with the same soggy summer I have. He's also the clergyman who will be officiating at the ceremony.

I explain about the front hallway and possible seating arrangements.

"Great idea," he says. "I'd figured it that way too. Just wanted to see if you were on the same page."

I am, and it pleases me because a.) he agrees with me and b.) he's done countless weddings.

Worry begets worry. We have bears nearby. They might detect the great menu we've selected and decide that our salmon smells heavenly, that our chicken would be much tastier than their usual grubs and ants crunch. I share this concern with my parents on the phone.

"You're having a band, right?" Dad says.

"Yeah."

"So don't worry about the bears. If they come, they'll be dancing bears. They'll have a great time. We'll all have a great time."

I close my eyes and imagine large black bears wearing neck ruffs of purple silk to match the bride. But the worry doesn't go away. As I weed each of the gardens, as I plant the pots that will line the parade route, I keep scanning the property for bears. I can only hope that Dad's right. That the band will be loud enough to keep all the wildlife away.

I could never possibly have imagined it, all those years ago. That instead of facing interpersonal chaos and fierce ancient grudges at my daughter's wedding, I'd be fretting about septic systems, thunderstorms, and bears.

☆

For six weeks, the preparations and plans go forth, and then the tempo accelerates. The bride and groom arrive, and so does the dress, handmade by my daughter's stepmother and delivered by her father. Hallelujah, it fits!

Friends and family travel from Scotland, Hungary, France, the West Coast, the Midwest, the Eastern Seaboard. The tent goes up and looks beautiful. No septic tanks will be harmed during the celebration of this wedding.

The pre-wedding parties begin—the guys disappear somewhere that includes much beer. The women kayak and picnic and arrange the table flowers picked from our gardens. A few small drops of rain splatter down, but quit before the rehearsal begins. A few tears also splatter down my cheeks, but only at the rehearsal. I get them out of my system quickly.

The wedding day dawns bright. We've chosen the only sunny Saturday of the summer thus far. The wine and beer arrive and so do the caterers. The wedding women depart to get fancy and I leave the worries behind. I am now in party mode.

At the proper time, our granddaughter rings the farm bell near the back door to kick off the wedding. She's been a flower girl twice and was hoping for a third turn, but she's nearly a foot taller than the bride. Instead of carrying a basket of petals, she's the official wedding starter—an office her younger brother has been bragging about. "My sister gets to start the wedding—the whole wedding." (Can you have a half wedding?)

The whole wedding is perfect. It is a family affair—my husband and the groom's sister play the music. His brother performs the

ceremony. Brothers and sisters of the bride and groom are attendants. We have a parade of grandparents, and the sun keeps shining
all day.

The bears don't attend—Dad was right and we all have a great
time. People play bocce and croquet. We eat wonderful food, drain
bottles and kegs. I nudge my ex-husband into asking his wife to dance,
which shocks her and earns me many points. But she made the wedding dress, so she deserves a dance or two. My nephew and grandson, rascals both, karate-dance as a twosome with as many ladies as
they can find, earning them even more points.

As we get to know the groom's parents, we bond and wish they
lived closer. I find it nostalgic and lovely to see people I used to call
sisters- and brothers-in-law, to meet their grown children whom
I've never seen but only heard about. It all feels like family. Our only
visible critters are the mosquitoes. The band sends out a song dedicated to them, and we line up three kinds of bug spray at the bar.

Later, I like to think, when I look back at the pictures, that maybe
a hundred yards or so into the woods, along the path back to the pond,
the bears were also having a good time. That with or without purple
ruffs or complicated family dynamics, they too may have danced at
my daughter's wedding.

We can judge the heart of a man by his treatment of animals . . .

—Immanual Kant

bad PR

ON THIS TRIP to the country during the summer after the wedding, a Saturday in late May, big trucks surround us on the highway. No one seems to have told them that we're in the middle of a recession, that folks aren't buying stuff at the usual rate. We have had a *bear market* on Wall Street for some time, so named for reasons that remain obscure. One theory suggests that bears are sluggish (and maybe they are when emerging from hibernation), while bulls charge forward. In fact, wide-awake-bears can run quite well, so this theory does not particularly persuade me.

A subtler notion comes from the ways these animals behave when on attack. The bull puts his head down and drives horns upward, while the bear may swing down with powerful, muscular forepaws and sharp claws. So the bull market implies an upswing while the bear represents a downswing. All of this sounds a little too convenient, too after-the-fact.

I prefer an historical theory, because I love to discover small tidbits from the past. Centuries ago, sellers of bearskins sometimes sold skins they didn't yet own, in hopes of making a profit if prices dropped when they actually purchased the hides. These middlemen became known as *bears,* and the term may have stuck for a down-turning market. And because bulls as well as bears were the victims of blood sports, perhaps bulls in finance were named as bears' opposites.

Regardless of the source of characterization, I find it a poor fit for my sense of these animals. Given a choice, I'd prefer to meet a bear unexpectedly, except as it relates to my retirement account. The bull will indeed have head down and be pawing the ground, ready to gore me with those sharp horns. I probably won't survive. The bear might grumble and posture, but will most likely turn and retreat, back to the honey tree. Hunger trumps aggression in black bears and I can walk away, trembling but intact. So I don't believe bears should portray such a negative economic image. It's bad P.R. for the species. They definitely need a spin-doctor.

☆

And then there's the Russian bear, shown in political cartoons as a vicious monster, especially during the days of the Cold War. This is a brown bear, *Ursus arctos,* a sub-species of *Caniform,* known for its large size. It is also a characterization that may insult both an animal and a country. For more than three centuries, political sketches have portrayed Russia as a bear—large, powerful, but bumbling and not too bright. Aggressive and needing to be tamed by stronger, wiser folk—the Lion of Great Britain, for example, or the Bald Eagle of the United States.

In many ways, this seems inappropriate. Forget bumbling. Bears are large and powerful, but they move gracefully and can operate on two legs as well as four. They're smart; they know how to protect their young and have long memories for food sources—and they've mastered various types of doorknobs and refrigerator latches. In 2010 a wildlife researcher captured photographs of an Alaskan brown bear picking up a barnacle-covered rock and using it to scrub and groom its muzzle—a wild bear using the rock as a tool—a skill we humans have mostly claimed for ourselves and other primates. Time to rethink our notions of the wisdom of bears.

As to ferocity, even though browns may be more aggressive than, say, my black bears, they're less threatening than either the Lion or the Bald Eagle, both fierce carnivores, and bears' diets are mostly vegetarian. If they do attack other animals it's most likely to be a nest of ants or grubs.

And if the Russians themselves were bumbling and not too bright, why were we so afraid of them for so many years in the mid-twentieth century? It makes absolutely no sense. In other parts of Europe, both Germany and Finland consider the bear to be their national symbol, but this seems to be a result of choice, rather than assignment.

Bears are also associated with Berserkers, fierce Norse warriors who raged and pillaged wearing animal skins, including those of bears. These warriors appear in epics and eddas with tempers hugely aroused —perhaps by ingesting huge amounts of alcohol, or psychedelic drugs. This ancient history gives us today's word, berserk, which means violently and destructively frenzied. Yet another negative image, if not for the bear, at least for his skin.

☆

Bears fare better in United States' iconography. Two states, California and Missouri, include images of bears (not black but grizzly) on their state flags and state seals. The California flag, approved in 1911, features a full-bodied grizzly bear down on four paws facing left against a white field. The image was modeled on an actual bear, Monarch, the last wild California grizzly in captivity. Captured in 1889 by news reporter Allen Kelley at the suggestion of William Randolph Hearst, the bear lived at the zoo at the Golden Gate State park until its death when it was stuffed and exhibited.

Missouri's flag, adopted in 1913, is even more pro-bear as it includes three ursine images. In the Show-Me state's seal at the flag's center, two mighty grizzly bears support a smaller central seal which includes three images: a crescent moon representing the young state; a bear representing strength and bravery; and a small version of the Great Seal of the United States. Strength and bravery sounds a lot better to my ear than violently and destructively frenzied like those Berserkers.

When it comes to state animals, bears again are somewhat popular. Grizzlies were chosen by California and Missouri, but four states selected black bears: New Mexico in 1963, West Virginia in 1973, Louisiana in 1992, and Alabama in 2006. While bears are populous in both New Mexico (6,000) and West Virginia (10,000), choosing a bear as the state animal for Louisiana (bear population 700) seems like wishful thinking. For Alabama (bear population 50) it seems clueless.

Alaska and Maine, both situated far to the north and at the continental extremes chose to represent themselves with moose, a burly selection. Massachusetts doesn't have a state animal but Pennsylvania joins ten other states (from New Hampshire to Nebraska) in honoring the white-tailed deer. Either that or there are just so many deer around that folks gave in to the electoral pressure and voted for the deer: *we'll make you our state animal if you promise not to devour our shrubs.*

I don't think it's working. Perhaps those deer have misinterpreted the mandate and believe their current assignment is to be fruitful and multiply—to spread small spotted fawns from sea to shining sea until every state selects the white tailed deer as its chosen beast. Kind of a deer-a-fest destiny. Sure, it's a weird notion, that doesn't usually stop anyone in expansionist mode.

Truly, I don't know what the deer are thinking, or if they're thinking. Perhaps the does and bucks do have a master plan, but they're not talking about it. Or maybe they are—maybe they're whispering their secrets to the bears, just not to us. Considering our history with various flora and fauna, I don't blame them.

*Until he extends his circle of passion to include all living
things, man will not himself find peace.*

—Albert Schweitzer

unbearable

SOME TIME HAS passed since I've seen a live bear, so I fire up my
laptop and go bear hunting. The first pictures I see include bears in
the wild—mothers with cubs, bears in trees, bears in winter, hunting shots—and numerous cartoons or drawings. I see a purported
bear-inflicted injury, plenty bloody, and even a Teddy Bear Hamster.
These small rodents, otherwise known as Syrian hamsters, *Mesocrice-
tus auratus,* have long, golden, fluffy fur. This bear would be fun to get
to know up close; it would fit in my palm.

I dig deeper and disturbing images emerge from the infinite gal-
axy of cyberspace. When I see the trained Russian circus bears playing hockey—and wearing hockey skates—I recognize the posture. I
can feel it in my knees.

When I was a small child, I loved to dress up. I'd put on an old
discarded nightgown and drape myself with filmy scarves, ropes of
costume jewelry. And then I'd put on a pair of my mother's high heels
and clomp around, off balance and teetering.

These poor hockey bears appear just as off-kilter, forced to remain upright for long periods of time with their large hind paws
stuffed into skates. In some photos a single skater-bear is passing the
puck to a human trainer. In others, a cluster of huge brown bears aim

slap shots at each other or at the goal nets. The bears are so large, they crowd the ice. It's creepy.

Some of the bears must think so too. In October 2009, one of these skating bears attacked two people and killed one of them, its trainer. While attacks are unusual, they aren't unheard of, which leads me to investigate further, to discover why a well-trained and somewhat tamed circus bear might turn vicious.

I continue to search the circus bear sites and find bears wearing bright skirts and ruffs. They jump over hurdles, balance on balls, walk on their front paws in handstand position, ride bikes and even motorcycles. Dancing bears hop in circles, play leapfrog, tumble, swing hula hoops around their necks, and swing dance with a woman partner.

The circus is an ancient form of entertainment, featuring both human and animal performers. These days, the humans have probably chosen this occupation. The animals certainly have not. In the wild, they'd own large territories. In the circus they live in constricted spaces and display stereotypic behaviors: pacing, head rolling, rocking, swaying from side to side, biting and self-mutilation.

Their performances—whether dancing or tumbling or biking — have been learned through extensive training. On the video, the trainer rewards the animal with a tidbit of food, but in fact, positive reinforcement is not the only training method.

On the Indian subcontinent today, dancing bears (cubs poached from the wild) are reportedly trained to *dance* much as Europeans trained captive bears in the Middle Ages—by coating the bears' feet with oil and forcing them to walk on hot metal surfaces while music plays. Or they are restrained and forced to dance by people whacking their feet while music plays or a drum beats. The bears soon learn to associate the music with the pain, and their *dancing* is really hopping, a result of painful, aversive conditioning.

This information jars me. I smile when I remember my own dancing lessons in sixth grade in the basement rec room of a classmate named Jimmy. We all gathered, with a teacher and Jimmy's approving mother, paired off in couples in hug position, and learned the proper steps. It was a chance to touch a boy, sweaty hand to sweaty hand, to feel his arm around me and if the dance was slow, to sense his heartbeat and wonder if he sensed mine. Anything but aversive—it was instead an initiation into heat, into the mysteries of what magical things might happen when we grew up. The lessons took—I still remember the dance steps and associate the music with joyfulness, not pain.

Those poor bears. Then again, their burgeoning sexuality doesn't require dancing lessons, or any particular locale, or supervision for expression and exploration. When bears in the wild are mature and ready, they find partners, play for a spell, and then mate, without, one hopes, the excruciating questions of human adolescence. *Will he? Does he? Can I? Should I?*

Performing bears though, their questions, if their minds form questions, must be more immediate and direct and pain-related: *why, and why me,* and *when will it hurt again?* Many have teeth and claws filed down or removed for the safety of the trainers. And some have holes burned from nose to forehead to insert a training rope, all without anesthetic. If this sounds particularly archaic, think again. In Eastern Europe incidents of dancing bears were reported as recently as 2007. Elsewhere, it is going on now. The photographs make me cringe.

There is some good news for performing bears these days. In the United States, industry-wide standards protect animals and prevent cruelty or abuse to the creatures that work for television and the movies. Bears are trained using positive rewards; they are fed tasty nibbles each time their behavior comes closer to that desired by the trainer until they can rear up on signal, or open their mouths and show a lot of teeth. The problem is, those aren't real bear behaviors—they exist primarily in the minds of the trainers hired to portray bears as wild and ferocious for the camera. So those images too, capture something ludicrous, something foolish and invented.

☆

Cameras hadn't been invented in Elizabethan times so there are no photos. If there were, we'd see in full color what now is only shown in black and white etchings: bear baiting, a so-called blood sport like cock fighting or dog fighting. [Baiting, as to tease, not to entice with food.] In bear baiting, a bear is enclosed in a pit and tied to a post with a small length of rope, which restricts its movement to a few feet in any direction. A pack of trained hunting dogs, Canis lupus familiaris, is let into the pit and spectators bet on the outcome, cheer for the dogs. Some dogs will receive a fatal blow with a heavy, clawed forepaw. Some will draw blood from the bear. Others, perhaps the most ferocious, will leap up, aiming for the jugular, for the kill.

Of the dogs, mastiffs (huge dogs), Staffordshire terriers, and English bull terriers (like Spuds McKenzie) were common breeds used in bear- and bull-baiting. With the English bulldogs, crowds came to prefer white coats over the reddish brindle colored dogs, as such a coloration offered better contrast and drama when bloody.

In England, herds of bears were kept for this sport, as well as packs of hounds, and it was a favorite of King Henry VIII, and of his daughter, Elizabeth I. Bear gardens, such as the famous Paris Garden at Southwick in London, flourished. The practice was condemned by the Puritans, those stiff-necked religious reformers who would one day settle my state of Massachusetts. Their condemnation seemed more connected to the fact that the bear baiting occurred on Sundays, the Sabbath, rather than to any animal cruelty involved.

When bears were in short supply, bulls would also be used to entertain. Then as now, the lives of bull calves were likely to be shorter than those of heifers. A single bull can service an entire herd of cows, so the extra male offspring would be either gelded and trained as oxen to the plow or raised for meat. Females would provide milk and increase the herd with calves, and so would be relatively better treated. The bulls used in baiting (and also the bears), once dead, would be taken to the butcher and end up at the table, much as the bulls used in bullfights do today. So it isn't surprising that these animals were killed, for we follow the same pattern today, gelding and then raising steers for the meat markets or hunting bears for the table. But the manner of the killing was bloody, dramatic and prolonged.

Only in 1835 did Parliament outlaw baiting. But again, as with shows of dancing bears, bear baiting continues in the present among nomadic tribes on the Indian subcontinent.

I can't fathom what leads a human being to abuse another living creature. And I question whether or not the blood sport of baiting is better or worse than the lifelong misery of performance. To me, they are both unbearable. I can only tolerate observing a finite number of animals experiencing mistreatment. I must look at these images in order to understand, but at a certain point, I shut down the computer and head outside to clear my mind of the evil.

I relish the soft, damp grass underfoot, the swooping flight of the goldfinches, *Carduelis tristis,* against the blue sky. Odd Latin name, though, for the finches. *Tristis* implies sadness when in fact the birds seem only joyful. On this day, the plop-plop of the frogs as I walk alongside the creek is perfect rhythm, perfect music. Even the raised tunnels of the small moles, *Talpidae,* that sometimes make me grumpy are cause for celebration. Here in this small corner, the earth is green and the animals are living their animal lives without toxic human interference. I try to observe quietly.

☆

The bears that travel with Gypsies are always called
"Brother Martin . . ."

—Robertson Davies

☆

what's in a name?

IN MY FIRST real job after college I worked as a teacher's assistant. My boss wasn't small and she didn't chirp, but her name was Cricket. I never knew if she had a real name. The grandfather of Amy, a Pittsburgh friend, used to call her Pooh Bear and she now calls her daughter June-Bug. My little granddaughter and I exchange a silly greeting when we first see each other after time apart: *Hey, Bug, Bug, Bug.* Giggles follow. Pet names are common endearments among families.

☆

In the creation story, Genesis chapter two, God fills the earth with fellow beings to keep the man company. He then charges the man with the task of naming them all. It's a good task for a talkative creature like *Homo sapiens,* and the man takes his work seriously. *You there, with the long neck, I'll call you giraffe. You, wagger, you'll be dog. And that little crawly one in the corner, he'll be cockroach. . . .* In an *urso*-centric world, the language might echo with words and phrases for berry, acorn, fresh leaves, grubs. But in our *Homo*-centric speech, we name everything we see and a number of things we can't: *cold front, existentialism, nano-second.* We even name ourselves, and then, as if regular names weren't enough, we christen ourselves with pet names, nicknames, even the occasional epithet.

☆

A Florida golf course near St. Augustine has an odd name—The King and The Bear. Part of World Golf Village, the course was designed by lifelong rivals Arnold Palmer (The King) and Jack Nicklaus (The Bear). The course adjoins another weirdly named course, The Slammer and The Squire, named for Sammy (The Slammer) Snead and Gene (The Squire) Sarazen. Golf nicknames are quirky.

Nicklaus' nickname may have come from his high school—the mascot of the Upper Arlington High School in Columbus, Ohio, is the Golden Bear. Or it may have come from an Australian sportswriter, Don Lawrence, who used the name to describe the hefty, blond golfer (previously tagged Fat Jack, and yeah, I'd rather be a Golden Bear than a Fat Jack). Whatever the source, the Golden Bear has stayed with Nicklaus throughout his long career.

Nicklaus isn't the only golfer to carry an animal name. Fans call Greg Norman the Great White Shark. And of course, there's Tiger Woods. His real name is Eldrick Tont Woods, but he was nicknamed Tiger to honor a friend of his father's. Hard to imagine hauling about a name like Eldrick Tont in one's golf bag, or even on the pages of tabloids. But then maybe his life would have been less complicated with his real name; maybe all the women he *entertained* would have been less interested in bedding an Eldrick than a Tiger.

Nor is Jack Nicklaus the only Bear out there. The Discovery Channel hosts survival expert Bear Grylls, chef Jamie Oliver named his son Bear, and her mother-in-law named actress Alicia Silverstone's son Bear Blu. Perhaps the most famous human Bear is Bear Bryant, legendary football coach of the University of Alabama's Crimson Tide. He reportedly earned his name by wrestling with a bear at age thirteen. Sounds scary. I'd like to see a photo, to know how big Bryant and that bear were at the time.

Many animal first names belong to men: politician and jurist Salmon P. Chase; showman Buffalo Bill Cody; rapper Snoop Dogg; warrior Crazy Horse; songwriter and guitarist Howling Wolf; baseball player Moose Skowron. Only one woman appeared on any of my various research lists: former first lady Claudia Alta, aka, Lady Bird Johnson. But former Alaska governor and presidential hopeful Sarah Palin, in addition to referring to herself as a Mama Grizzly, was called Sarah Barracuda earlier in life due to her highly aggressive style of basketball play. Fans used the name as a compliment; opponents did not.

There are a lot of Jays out there, and several Kittys, clearly derivatives of actual first names, John and Katherine respectively (but not *this* Katherine, thank you). Singer Cat Stevens presents an interesting case—born Steven Demetre Georgiou, he took on Cat Stevens as a stage name and then later changed it legally to Yusuf Islam. A man in motion, repeatedly redefining himself. In my town of Pittsburgh, a gregarious bar owner and town character was much beloved: Froggy Morris, so named because of his deep, gravely, bassoon of a voice.

Theophilis Eugene Bull Connor made news in Birmingham, Alabama during the early days of the Civil Rights Movement. Bull Connor was the politician and city official behind the infamous police incidents where police aimed fire hoses at peaceable demonstrators, all caught on film, both still and news clips. A lifelong Ku Klux Klan member, he must have been dismayed to discover that his actions, instead of stopping the protests, actually increased national sympathies for the movement and may have helped smooth the passage of Civil Rights legislation.

The world of fiction offers a few more notable animal names: John Updike's Rabbit Angstrom; TV classic Beaver Cleaver; John Wayne's memorable Rooster Cogburn; Crocodile Dundee, a.k.a. Paul Hogan; and of course, the unforgettable female lead in the James Bond film *Goldfinger,* Pussy Galore. Ironically for ladies' man Bond, she's a lesbian in the film. Pinocchio's friend Jiminy Cricket really was a cricket so he doesn't count.

☆

When we name animals after ourselves, or give them human characteristics, we call that anthropomorphism. I wonder what the critters
think of us borrowing their names. Animopomorphism perhaps. I'm
pretty sure they'd object to our use of their names as insults or pejo-
ratives, just as I flinch when someone refers to a person as *such a Chatty
Cathy*. I take this misuse of my name personally as I am: a.) chatty and
b.) Kathy.

One of my father's preferred descriptions of his mother is that
she drove like a bat out of hell, but most times he reports this as a
compliment, rather than an insult. Last I checked actual bats live not
in Hades, but in caves, or occasionally in my attic—but no, I don't
think I have bats in my belfry.

Animal insults are nothing new—Shakespeare used them—*vile
worm, puppy-headed monster, Thou bitch-wolf's son*. In *A Midsummer Night's
Dream* he turned Bottom into an ass. But he was a master of the language, so his insults sound fresh; they sing on the page or stage, or even
dance, in the case of poor Bottom.

Contemporary insults seem more prosaic. I admit to being *bos
taurus*-headed; some would say I take pride in it. I've been called a
Caridea (shrimp) and probably a female *Canis lupus familiaris*, but not
to my face. Given a choice, I prefer that *C-l-f*, which has more spirit,
to cur (sounds like a guy) or dog, as in really ugly girlfriend material.
I wouldn't mind being *Vulpes* (a fox)—especially at this grandma time
of life—but you'd ruffle my fur if you called me *Soricidae* (mousy or
shrewish) or *Annelida* (a leech) or *Cetacea* (a whale) or a *Hippopotamus
amphibious* or a *Suidae* (pig). And I repeat, I am Katherine, Kathy, very
occasionally Katy, but *never* Kitty or Kitten. *Meow, hiss, scratch.* For
me, feathered insults seem pretty insipid—*Gallus gallus domesticus,
Pavo cristatus, Meleagris,* (chicken, peacock, turkey). Who cares? But I
admire *Bufonidae, Serpentes,* and *Oligochaeta* (toad, snake, and worm),
particularly satisfying as put-downs.

I try to understand this, why we call ourselves and other people
by animal names. We may be seeking affiliation, a connection with

nature, a large dose of cuteness. That seems possible with the family pet names. The insults too seem pretty straightforward—we can diminish someone by lowering his status on the evolutionary pecking order, *you Mustela (weasel), you.*

In Brazil, according to local jokes, animal nicknames change over time. Before marriage, one might call the beloved by a small animal name, my bunny, my puppy. After marriage, the names refer to big beasts—you cow, you pig!

Even more curious is the phenomenon of adopting an animal's name as part of one's own persona. Perhaps we do this (and yes, sorry, but it is more common among males) to inflate our egos, to add machismo and bring the power of the chosen animal into our own lives.

But seriously, Catfish *(Siluriformes)* Hunter. That either means the guy was a bottom feeder or that he fished a lot. And Goose *(Anatidae)* Goslin a long-necked depositer of manure. Okay, Goose makes sense with his odd last name. But Newt Gingrich? For more reasons than I can count, that will never make sense. I prefer the red-spotted newts, *Salamandridae,* I find in the woods anyway.

Those who wish to pet and baby wildlife love them, but those
who respect their natures and wish to let them live their
natural lives, love them more.

—Edwin Way Teale

wild thing, you make my heart sing . . .

IN *WHERE THE Wild Things Are,* Maurice Sendak sends his hero Max "to
the place where the wild things are." Sendak's book, which came out
in 1963, caused quite a stir. Adults believed the wild things would
frighten children beyond belief. Instead, the children loved them,
loved the book, and generations later, they still do. Sendak was wise
in so many ways—in knowing how children understand wildness perhaps better than adults do, in his transformation of his childhood
ogres (his actual elderly relatives) into monsters, but particularly in
his choice to send Max into the wild things' territory instead of the
other way around.

Some time ago, I met a fellow writer who had adopted a young
black bear. The two-month-old cub had been orphaned and used for
research but at some point his claws had been removed, so he could
not have survived in the wild. The placement of choice was an animal
preserve, but in all likelihood, over time the bear would have grown
too large and too wild and would have been put down.

The man hated the thought, but he didn't take on the responsi-
bility of parenting a bear cub lightly. He lived in Montana, and owned
enough land so that if he adopted the bear, both the animal and the
surrounding humans would be safe. He studied bear research, filled

out stacks of paperwork and permits until finally he could bring the 20-pound cub home. There, he built a habitat including a shelter, pond, and play space. Then the serious work began. The writer spent hours each day feeding and nurturing the cub. This continued for months. As the cub grew larger, his mischief increased proportionally, but so did his attachment to his human friend. This story has a happy ending—the bear became a part of the writer's family and lived with them for twenty-seven years until his death. A long life for a bear, and a good life.

☆

Not all such stories have happy endings. During the fall of 2011, Zanesville, Ohio and the rural land nearby became the site of a large wild-animal massacre. There, a man and his wife had assembled a collection of exotic animals, which they kept in cages and displayed at various events, fairs, gatherings.

The man, Terry Thompson, had a history of instability, and in October he took his own life, but not before releasing all the animals on his farm. Most of the animals left their cages and roamed the countryside, frightening the nearby communities. Schools closed and people were advised to stay indoors until sheriff's deputies could hunt down, shoot and destroy the creatures.

They killed forty-nine in total—six black bears, eighteen Bengal tigers, seventeen lions, one baboon, two grizzly bears, three mountain lions and two wolves. One monkey went missing, and was presumed to have been eaten by one of the larger predators. Six animals did not choose to leave their cages. They survived and were sheltered at the Columbus Zoo, but then in April, 2012, Thompson's wife reclaimed her *pets,* and returned them to the same farm—two leopards, two monkeys and a bear. A third leopard had been housed at the zoo, but didn't survive.

☆

It's hard to imagine a private couple taking charge of fifty-six wild and exotic animals. There isn't enough time in a day for the kind of care and nurture the Montana writer gave to a single bear cub. It's also hard to imagine assembling such a collection—but sure enough live auctions and online sources offer wild and exotic animals for sale, often young cubs.

Big cats are particularly popular—lions, tigers, leopards, cougars. Estimates run as high as fifteen thousand exotic cats living as pets in the United States. Similarly, primates become frequent pet choices, and they too number about fifteen thousand.

Most are bought when young, cute and cuddly with little thought to public safety or animal welfare. The problems arise when they grow to full maturity and the owners have more on their hands than they can manage. At that point, some owners try to place the animal in a zoo or preserve but such environments often operate at full capacity and have no room for additions to their populations. A frustrated owner might neglect the animal or become casual in caretaking. Even well-tended animals sometimes escape and frighten neighbors or cause traffic jams when crossing a busy highway. Some wild pets end up attacking people, others are found dead at the side of the road.

Reptiles are even more popular than the cats and primates. More than seven million snakes, alligators, crocodiles, and other reptiles live in cages in people's homes in the United States. Some of the owners are young children. And some of the snakes are deadly—venomous puff adders, homegrown copperheads and rattlers, or constrictor varieties, like Burmese pythons or boas, which when fully grown may reach twenty feet in length. The child owner may be about four feet tall.

And yes, accidents do happen. When the reptiles grow too big to manage, owners often just let them go free. In the north, if the creatures are exotics, winter's cold will kill them. But in warm climates? Everglades National Park now has a resident population of Burmese pythons—a breeding population of an invasive species that is growing. Wildlife officers don't believe they can uproot this species; they simply hope to control it if possible, to keep it from spreading.

When a young animal is orphaned in the wild, a number of consequences exist: the animal may survive or it may die, due to starvation or predation; the animal may be caught and sold; the animal may be rescued and returned to the wild by a skilled wildlife rehabilitator; the animal may be housed in a preserve or in a zoo where it may be exhibited and where its needs will be met and its life may benefit others of its kind.

I admire wild animals but their essential state is wildness; I believe humans should respect that. So while I applaud the writer for his devotion to his bear, I'd prefer that the bear had lived a true bear's life in the wild. Ironically, the writer himself agrees, warning about the dangers to humans and to the animals of making wild creatures into pets. And yet he was extremely attached to his bear.

Michael Webber, director of *The Elephant in the Living Room,* a documentary film about exotic pets, believes that most owners of exotics feel the same way. While owners of domestic animals love their pets, Webber believes that owners of wild animals love theirs more—five or ten times more. The larger and more powerful the animal, the larger and more powerful the bond the owner forges with them. He also attributes the growth of exotic pet ownership during the past several years to reality television shows, which portray human/animal interactions in a dramatic and intense manner. *Whoa, cool. I could do that . . .*

And so it continues and grows, despite the dangers to people and to the animals themselves. There are more tigers in captivity in Texas than wild tigers in India. There are more fatal exotic animal incidents in the United States than in Africa, where many of the animals originate. People there have the wisdom to leave the creatures alone— they know they can be deadly and are sensibly afraid. And yet here thirty states allow people to keep exotic pets; nine require no licenses or permits. Owners argue that responsible ownership and careful tending prevent accidents. They advocate for the personal freedom to make their own choices.

☆

In perhaps the oddest incarnation of *lions and tigers and bears, oh my,* a Bengal tiger, a lion, and a black bear were captured in Georgia by police during a drug bust in 2001. The drug dealers had chosen to amplify their own macho personae by adopting the three young cubs. This story has a happy, if surprising, ending.

At the time of rescue, the three cubs, aged two months, had already become something of a family. So the Noah's Ark Rescue Center in Locust Grove, Georgia, decided to keep the animals together, despite the fact that in the wild they would not have coexisted happily if at all.

This same rescue center cares for abused or orphaned human children and they live on the campus with the orphaned animals. The children and the animals bond together and as the children help tend the animals, small and large, they learn to give and receive love. The children's center also functions as an adoption agency and facilitates the finding of "forever homes" for the children. Likewise, the domestic animals at the center may be "adopted" which means that individuals and groups may provide food and habitat support while the animals continue to live at the center.

After years at Noah's Ark, Baloo the bear, Shere Khan the tiger, and Leo the lion live like brothers in a specially designed habitat where they eat, sleep and play together—a modern day peaceable kingdom.

It's an unnatural wonder. Or perhaps not. When given the chance, even large predatory animals can learn to co-exist, and become friends. The real wonder is why some of us humans have such a hard time with each other, why we must argue and struggle and fight. I think there's a name for that too—when we behave badly. In a word, it's just plain beastly of us.

a war zone

MEMORIAL DAY WEEKEND, we arrive in the country to meet our newest tenant, Dina, who moved in earlier in the week. We also meet her tall, trim husband who will soon be shipping out to Afghanistan for a year. They're still settling her in and, oddly, they've shoved an old desk up against the door to the cottage's basement garage.

"How's it going?"

"Pretty well, but we did have a couple of problems," Dina says. "The movers made a mess of the driveway and trucks got stuck in the lawn. We've called the insurance company."

It is a mess; mud oozes everywhere. The driver had plenty of dry driveway to use, but for some reason rolled off the drive and had to be winched out by another huge truck, so ruts and tracks abound.

"It's fixable," I say. "Is everything all right with the cottage?"

Dina shrugs and looks uneasy. "The cottage is fine, but our second night here we heard a lot of noise."

"Bears got into the garage," the husband explains. "A mother and two small cubs. She must have smelled the garbage cans. We hollered and yelled, but it was really hard to get them to leave."

"And once they did leave, she came around to the front door and tried to get in that way," Dina says. "We didn't scrub off the marks so you could see."

I look closely at the garage door and see scratches and signs of forced entry. Now I understand why the lumpy old desk sits there; it's a barricade. At the front door, more evidence. Mama Bear has left muddy smears. Clearly Dina expects me to do something about all this, but I'm not sure exactly what.

"They also tried to get into your Dumpster," she continues. "I think that's what brought them to the property in the first place."

This isn't our first bear sighting at the house and cottage, and I tell them so. An early tenant spotted bears frequently and woke one morning to find the outline of a large, heavy bear rubbed into the dust on the side of his big black truck. The bear shape showed dark and shiny and clean; the rest of the truck needed a wash. Our rental agent was supposed to have warned them about all this and indeed she did, but still I worry.

As we return to our house, where the kitchen is under renovation, I spot two clear paw prints on the large green Dumpster. My contractor assures me that neither he nor any of his guys have put a single food wrapper or empty coffee cup in the Dumpster, but still the bear tried to climb up and investigate. Dumpsters are, after all, the *Ursine* equivalent of a trendy restaurant.

This incident seems significant enough that we report it to the local police, who ask to be informed if we see these animals again. They'll send out the wildlife police to trap and remove. That sounds wonderfully sensible, although removal doesn't always work. Bears have been known to return to their own territories even after being relocated many miles away in closed trucks. Their noses must be incredibly sensitive.

☆

The world can be strange. My neighbor Dina has moved back home to western Massachusetts to be safe and supported, close to family, while her husband travels to Kabul in the midst of a war zone. Under most circumstances, she'd be worrying about him. But with bears who've already broken in once, the worry gets flip-flopped. He frets about her from half a world away.

Her summer grows more complicated and her vulnerability increases. Her aunt dies unexpectedly. A sister gives birth. And in the midst of our watching out for bears, a frightening storm hits the property early one Wednesday evening—either a micro-burst or a mini-tornado. Both Dina and I are alone in our houses when the winds strike.

The winds are strong enough I must leave the sun porch—it feels too exposed—and so I head for the library, sprawling on the sofa with a book. Unfortunately, the sofa sits against a wall of windows on the north side of the house, the very direction from which the winds are blowing. The storm rattles the windows and sets up a hum that puts me on alert. If it gets really nasty, one of those windows could shatter.

It's only eight, but the sky has gone dark and I yearn for the comfort of my bed. More importantly, my bedroom faces south, out of the wind. Book in hand, I hurry upstairs and get into my jammies, as if somehow this comforting, settling-in ritual will make the wind settle down too. I re-open the book and lose myself in a bit of light fiction. I hear nothing, no rattles, no hums, and so relax a bit.

Twenty minutes later the phone rings. "Hello, are you all right?" My neighbor from across the highway is calling.

"Yes. I'm fine. Why?"

"Oh, the storm," she says. "All these trees have come down. The road is blocked. My husband is out checking on things."

When she says that, I notice the flicker of a flashlight out the window. And I'm in my jammies. I quickly pull on jeans, grab my own flashlight and race back downstairs where I hear the neighbor man calling my name.

I hurry out to meet him, but find it difficult to orient myself—my usual landmarks seem to have moved. Trees are down everywhere and the state police are now closing the highway to all traffic until workers can clear away the debris. I have heard none of this. Either I fell asleep or else it was a really good book. The house is sturdy; built in the 1920s, it has withstood hundreds of New England storms. This time it protected me from all danger.

Soon Dina joins us and we aim our three small beams of light at the chaos. "Do you think it was a tornado?" she asks. "I went down to the basement right away."

Smart woman. I went upstairs instead. Totally ridiculous. Back inside again, I phone my husband and he's not home, so my sense of vulnerability increases. Finally I reach him, and he's sympathetic, but can he do little from four hundred miles away.

The weather channel warns of another windstorm approaching later—at around ten. This time I'll be sensible. I pack up spare clothes, water, some snacks, the flashlight, my cell phone and laptop, and hide out in the built-in bench under the main stairway. It's a good sturdy spot, and close to the basement door if I need to go down.

The second storm never arrives. Later, after much reading, I fall asleep upstairs to the music of chain saws and of front loaders that scrape heavy logs off the pavement outside my bedroom windows again and again.

By morning's light I discover that six huge old trees have been blown down on our land, two uprooted, the rest snapped like Tinkertoys in the hands of an angry child. It looks like a war zone. Dina and I are fortunate, however, as neither of us has experienced harm to ourselves, to our houses, or to our vehicles, although one monster tree missed my back bumper by a mere foot.

Two of my gardens now lie crushed under great, heavy trunks and branches of grand old white pines, *Pinus strobus.* I can barely stand to look outdoors in any direction. Devastation surrounds me except in the front garden, which I'd just finished tending the morning before the storm. The house protected the front landscape from damage, so when I'm feeling stressed by the mess everywhere else, I stroll the front walk and admire the delicate tree peonies, *Paeonia suffruticosa,* still bearing their pink dinner-plate-sized blooms. It seems so odd— huge trees crashed down and the peonies haven't dropped a petal.

The sound of that wind—a high-pitched keening—stays in my ears for days. And, while I mostly love living with wildness on three sides of the property, I love the wildness of bears and birds, of snapping turtles and frogs. And I prefer them outside. I've had inside my various homes at various times these unwelcome visitors: a suburban squirrel; an urban rat; a green snake; a flyover bat; and many, many mice, of both city and country tribes. This is not the wildness I covet, nor do I yearn for the wildness of fierce winds.

Perhaps I want my nature served up in manageable doses—a peek at the bear, a moment when we coexist in the same territory but don't actually come face to face, a moment when I can look large and back away to my own den. Looking large in the face of howling winds is not an optimal survival strategy. *You've become a bigger target? All the better to blow you away, my dear.*

Poor Mama Bear. I suddenly wonder how she survived the storm. *If* she survived the storm. During the warm months, black bears often select resting spots near large trees, especially white pines, whose rough bark makes climbing easy. If danger approaches mother and cubs can scamper up the tree. For reasons of safety sometimes the bear family will sleep for the night, high in the branches. At other times, the mother will leave her cubs in a tree for a spell while she goes off to forage or mark territory.

Surely this mother bear had one or more of these bedding trees; white pines are common here. So I wonder about her trees, if one blew over or fell on someone. I hope her property has survived intact, and her family. I can't imagine how she managed with two small cubs to protect, cubs, like small children, afraid of the storm. Did she go up, as I foolishly did when the winds howled? Or was she smart, like my neighbor, heading for lower elevations during the storm?

And then there's Dina. I'm feeling wrecked and my family is safe; nobody lives in a war zone. I shiver when I think how she must be feeling. I can't imagine it.

☆

The greatest thrill is not to kill but to let live . . .

—James Oliver Curwood

☆

what needs to be done

SOON AFTER THE storm, the lawn guy comes to mow those parts of the yard not covered in branches. When he arrives, both Dina and I head outside. Nothing like a natural disaster in a small town to make people want to share the newest news. Everyone who stops by offers support, friendship, gossip.

The lawn guy's been removing limbs and branches from properties all over the area, many with punctured roofs, broken skylights, battered walls. The neighborhoods by the town pond have been particularly devastated and the crew from the power company sends all other emergency workers away in order to secure and repair the many downed electrical lines. So lots of workmen are free to come work on my house this morning.

In fact, ten men in trucks show up at the house in a single day, and five of them are named Rick. This seems incredibly odd: Rick the contractor, Rick the lawn guy, Rick the electrician, Rick the plumber, Rick the assistant to our property manager. All of the guys, the Ricks, plus the other five variously named fellows are kind and concerned. Each assures me that if more trouble comes, I should phone immediately.

It is a safety net and I appreciate it. Earlier in the summer I've watched some of them offering assistance to my young neighbor in that way men have of being protective of women they deem vulnerable. But a part of me pulls back—I don't want to seem vulnerable. Don't want to be that older woman by herself in the big house. No, I want to be the hiker, kayaker, gardener. I want to be (and mostly am) the woman who knows how to operate a drill—who can hammer a sheet of plywood across her own broken window should it be necessary. But I also admit, I hope it won't be necessary.

Still these men and their concern make me feel connected, a part of the community. As a part-timer, I haven't yet made many friends in the area. That will happen when we spend more time here, but for now, my local friends and acquaintances are mostly these workmen and contractors. So I want their camaraderie, not their pity.

This feels oddly familiar and then I realize. When I was a child my pals were the boys and I could count on them to run about, climb trees, play baseball. I learned the rules of physical games and sports much earlier than the queen bee rules of who's in and who's out and why or why not which never quite made sense in my mind. A perennial puzzle, to this day.

Here though, in the storm's aftermath, I can count on these guys, perhaps not to show up with a ball and bat, but with hammer and drill and chain saw as needed. Although I could, I don't have to manage all this alone, for they are worrying about me, and about Dina. It is a comfort.

☆

Dina has her own news to report. Bear scat a few yards from the garage door. She points it out. First thing, you notice that bear scat is huge—the size of a football.

"I can just see that bear, sitting there, watching me, watching my house."

Her voice trembles—I hear it.

The lawn guy nods to his young assistant who hurries to the truck for a shovel, clears up the mess, and carries it into the woods where it can decompose without worrying anyone. Then he asks me a question that surprises me, although it shouldn't. "Do I have your permission to do what needs to be done here?"

It takes me a moment. I close my eyes to the vision of a mother with two cubs. Cute cubs who might not be old enough to survive on their own. Who might be afraid of big storms. I opt for a delaying tactic. "Do you have . . . what you'd need? If . . . if those bears come back?"

"I always have what I need. I work outdoors in wilder places than this. I'm always ready."

I've known he was a woodsman and a good one. But these words cause me to stare at his truck momentarily. I haven't before imagined him packing heat. That he knows how to handle a rifle—sure. No surprise there; I've always assumed he was a hunter. But that he keeps a gun in his truck at all times—new information. It makes me uneasy and at the very same time, it feels safe.

My mind quickly scans the possibilities. Capturing and relocating —it doesn't always work. And besides, by the time we call the town police and they call the wildlife police, the bears will be long gone. They might not return for a week, a month, a season. Or if captured, they might return right away.

We can make sure all food and garbage is out of range—but we do this already and the bears have come back. I try to untangle the options, but it will take more time than I have just now. Dina needs an answer. I lose sleep when a bat flies overhead across the sun porch, when I discover mice nesting in my basement. She's had bears—three of them.

Then I blink, and for a moment it's not Dina standing before me. It's one of my daughters, alone in a new place, frightened and vulnerable. The choice is made.

"Yes," I tell him, a heavy weight in my chest. "You have my permission to do what needs to be done."

does the bear . . .

ON A FAMILY trip, I stop at the Pennsylvania Welcome Center, just across the West Virginia state line to use the restroom. Once finished with the facilities, I march out right into the information room, filled with maps and brochures and with a kindly looking woman staffing the desk. A medium-sized black bear guards the doorway. It's a real bear, at least it was. Now it's stuffed.

I can't resist. I reach out and scratch its head. Touch the thick fur on its left shoulder. Then I pull back my hand in surprise. The live bears I've seen wear shiny coats, so I've expected silkiness, something like a mink coat only thicker, or softness, like the fleece of an alpaca. Instead the bear's fur is coarse, almost gritty to the touch. That could be a result of the taxidermy chemicals, or the hundreds of other hands, some small and grimy, that have said hello to this bear. I want this roughness to be an artifact, manmade, but won't conclude that until I've done some searching.

As it turns out, a bear wears a two-layered coat. The outer guard hairs protect the bear from bumps, insects, scratches. The inner fur is softer and provides most of the insulating warmth. Unfortunately for the bears, that warmth is popular—websites offer up Canadian bear rugs for between $1,500 and $2,500. That's a rug made of a single skin with paws still attached, head in place, mouth gaping open as if ready to bite off somebody's foot. No thanks. Prettier, but still creepy, are the rectangular bear fur carpets without heads or feet. These cost between $6,000 and $10,000 depending on size. Made from spring pelts (because the fur is thicker) these carpets shine in the light. The true connoisseur can even purchase a silver fox blanket, which *coordinates well with the bear carpet*. Double no thanks.

Yes, I understand the notion of blankets—you throw one over yourself to stay warm. In the old days, people used bearskin rugs (blankets) to stay warm while riding in a sleigh over fields of snow. Understandable. But a fur rug or carpet—not in my house. My hardwood floor doesn't shiver in the winter. It doesn't need a bearskin jacket.

All these bear thoughts at a public rest area brings to mind the old jokes—Is the Pope Catholic? Does the bear . . . ? Well, yes, to both. I've seen bear scat in the woods, close up, if not the Pope. Him I've only seen in film or photographs. But of course the more whimsical questions switch things around. "Is the bear Catholic? Does the pope . . . ?

☆

As a child I found bathrooms endlessly fascinating. Whenever we arrived at a new destination, I automatically needed to use the facilities. This caused my mother great distress, because of the filthy conditions of most public restrooms. Once we arrived in the stall and slid the lock, she'd wallpaper the toilet seat to protect my little bum from any and all stray germs. Heaven help us if the T.P. roll was used up. She'd whip out the Kleenex, which she always carried in her purse. It was quite a show, actually. Perhaps I enjoyed having her fuss over me. Whatever the reason, my father took to calling me the B.R.I.— the bathroom inspector. I did have my standards, however. When confronted with an outhouse of any sort, I could magically hold my water for hours. The smells drove me away. That and the possibility of falling in. Help!

This bathroom interest has made its way down through the DNA, much to my daughter's chagrin. My youngest granddaughter has a new favorite thing—the porta-potty. As we drive along past highway construction sites, she calls out. "There's a porta-potty. A yellow one. There's a blue. Another one, it's white." Her mother groans. I giggle. This little girl likes to count, so at a farm-park she counts fifty-six porta-potties in a row, doubling the actual number. I hear joy and excitement in her voice as she reports all this on the phone.

As funny as it is, I don't really like porta-potties, as they closely resemble those nasty one- two- or three-holers that scared me off as a child. The chemicals don't really mask the odor. I sympathize with my daughter who had to visit one of these facilities in rural Vermont three times in one morning. Yuck.

The little one must have reasons for her interest, however. First off, the small plastic houses may look like play houses, just her size, a sort of Barbie Dream Home, toilet version. More importantly, these facilities don't have those nasty automatic flushers you find in high-way rest stops or restaurants. Those guys are a potent danger to every small-bottomed person who perches on the seat, for without warning they will roar and swirl, and might even suck you down into the vile sewers. Porta-potties are much safer—they don't flush at all, so they can't grab you and disappear you into the bowels of the earth. But the real attraction? In her own words, she likes to check out all those *old poopies*. Well, there are plenty to choose from.

☆

Bathroom humor, it seems, has been with us for a long time. There is the highly popular *Captain Underpants* series of books for children. Or the stories of *Walter, the Farting Dog*. There are endless varieties of birthday greeting cards for old men featuring noxious gasses. We laugh when a person leaves the private space of a bathroom for a more public locale trailing a streamer of toilet paper behind. Farm boys in my father's generation took great delight in privy tipping—and tipping was even more fun if the outhouse had an occupant at the time.

☆

Back in the days when indoor plumbing was new, many housewives were skeptics. *You're going to do that nasty business in my house? Think again. Take it outside where it belongs.*

Bears are much more naturalistic. They do just that: they use the woods. Or my lawn, several times this summer. I get to check out all those *old poopies.* Big ones. Lucky me.

At least the piles don't generally smell bad—like those outhouses or porta-potties do. A computer scientist/robotics engineer acronym comes to mind in this regard—*GIGO: garbage in, garbage out*—which describes attempts to locate the blame for a technological malfunction. The computer is most likely not at fault; it's the person sitting at the keyboard who made an error. For purposes of bear scat, I'd modify the meaning somewhat. Food group in, food group out—intake determines output.

If the bear has eaten berries, the scat will smell of berries. If she's visited the orchard, it will smell of apples and seeds will show up if I look closely. On another day it might smell of beechnuts and contain occasional bits of shell. But if she's been out chewing on that skunk cabbage, I need to stand back. It will likely smell of skunk.

Then again, bears, with their highly sensitive noses, probably find our outhouses and porta-potties rather noxious as well. Most parks and national forest sites have networks of bathroom facilities, many without benefit of running water. Bears must think us strange. We gather our wastes in small houses and save them up, as if they're treasure. As if the small houses are shrines to excrement.

You're going to do that nasty business in my forest? Think again . . .

☆

Animals do feel like us, also joy, love, fear and pain but they
cannot grasp the spoken word. It is our obligation to take
their part . . ."

—Denis de Rougement

☆

whose tree?

I STAND AND stare at the ruins of my most beautiful garden. Days
after the massive storm hits the Berkshires I am still shaken. Six trees
down in our yard, including one spectacular white pine with three
branching trunks, a hundred feet tall, that stood sentinel at the edge
between yard and wetland.

Some call the wind a micro-burst; some call it a tornado. I call
it terrifying when the winds reach a speed that produces a high
pitched, singing sound. I wanted to hide when it happened and I
want to hide now. I was attached to those trees—they were part of
what made this house home for me. I don't have the decades left in
my life that would be required for such giants to grow here again.

The sky is blue and cloudless—what my husband calls *a hundred
dollar bottle of wine sort of day.* The natural world seems bucolic and
benign, only a light soft breeze ruffles my hair. It hardly seems possible for that same sky to have poured out such devastation.

I survey the damage and take pictures, which I then send to various family and friends. My older daughter replies first. "That's Rob's
tree isn't it? He'll be so sad." Rob is a painter and has painted landscapes, which include that tree, so yes, he has a claim.

In my reply, however, I mention that I thought it was my husband's tree, as he climbed up with a ladder to remove dead branches and stubs, to give the tree its particularly graceful shape.

My younger daughter then weighs in. "That was our tree. The tree we were looking at when we got married. And now it's gone!"

"Yes, but you have the painting Rob made of that tree during the week of the wedding. And now it's a totally unique wedding. Nobody else can ever be married in front of that tree again."

This daughter, a botanist and plants-woman who understands the cycle of growth and decay, laughs.

A couple of days later I have the occasion to speak with the previous owner of our house and with her daughter.

"We were so sorry to see the big old tree come down," the older woman says.

Her daughter shakes her head. "That was the tree-house tree."

So even before our family grew attached to the old white pine, another family claimed and loved it.

About a week after the storm, my husband's brother comes to visit with his family. Our nephew can't wait to climb up along the downed trunk and proclaim himself king of the universe. He drags both parents up with him and their feet stand higher than my head.

Then our son and his family come to visit. The older children take a look and wander off to follow their own interests. The youngest grandson is very excited to see such an enormous tree lying on the ground; its root-ball rises more than twenty feet into the air, pretty tall for a little boy.

My daughter-in-law takes one look and says, "Oh no! It fell on our garden!" And indeed it did, for the women and children of the family planted this garden several years ago.

But the little guy can't stop musing about that big old tree. "How did it get so big down there on the ground?"

"It didn't. It got big up in the sky, and then it fell." I see from his frown that my answer doesn't fully satisfy him, but he has more questions.

"What are you going to do with it?"

I have no idea, except that I'd like to get it hauled away. Because it's pine, it's not a good bet for the fireplace. Too much pine sap equals creosote equals chimney fires.

"You could make furniture, Grandma. You could make a table and then a chair and another chair, and maybe another table."

I smile and shake my head, pleased that in his eyes, at least, I'm strong and powerful enough to tangle with such a huge hunk of tree.

But yes, we're all sorry to see such a majestic tree come to the end of its life. And a part of me worries what we'll find when the trunk is lifted off—how much of the garden will survive. But I can't worry too much. No people, no buildings, no cars were harmed in the tree-fall. And the garden plants have strong roots. They can sustain injury and re-grow.

☆

After my guests leave, but before the chain saws arrive, I wonder about other owners of the big white pine. American robins used to perch on the branches and chirp down at me, surrounded by feathery soft needles. They're now consigned to dirt and gnarly root and rock, if they perch there at all. How ugly it must seem to them, how harsh against their feet. If anyone had a nest there, eggs brooding, or new chicks just hatching, that's gone, all of it gone.

And the cottontail rabbits. The family garden now crushed by the pine was prime rabbit habitat. They nibbled on some of my perennials and shrubs, and hid amongst thick, low-growing branches. In previous years I've seen signs of rabbit nests—small depressions in the mulch with soft fur linings. Baby bunnies could have been struck by the huge trunk when it crashed to the ground. It happened at night, so they'd have gone to nest when darkness fell. Or perhaps the doe rabbit, so cagy at dodging the red tail, *Buteo jamaicensis,* and protecting her babies, was caught unprepared for this monster from the sky.

This pine tree and garden were visited by field mice, *Apodemus sylvaticus,* and squirrels. Cones will never again ripen here, nor provide endless seeds to fill their small bellies.

And finally, the bears. This could have been one of the signal trees—with deep scratches or nips in the bark—that marked an edge of territory. It could have served as a signpost for the bear that she'd nearly reached her den. She might have climbed it herself, or stashed a cub there for safety once upon a time.

So whose tree was it really?

It belonged to all of us—the people and animals who lived nearby and used or enjoyed it. Who sheltered, or nested, or perched, or nibbled or admired. To those in the present and those in the past. It belonged to the earth from which it grew, and to which it will now return as the process of decay begins. A good long life for a beautiful tree.

Amen. Which my older grandson would carefully remind me, means, *so be it.* A wise boy.

☆

Eat food. Not too much. Mostly plants.

—Michael Pollan

☆

hunter gatherer

I'M SITTING HERE at the computer wearing a shirt covered in colorful hand-drawn vegetables. The shirt is a souvenir from an extended book tour with one of my picture books for children—*Up, Down, and Around*—which features veggies and how they grow. (Yep, up, down, and around.) The drawings on my shirt were created and signed by young children in a small town in Pennsylvania where I was traveling to promote books and literacy, and incidentally to encourage healthy eating habits: Carrots, *Daucus carota*; peas, *Pisum sativum*; beets, *Beta vulgaris*; pumpkins, *Cucurbita*; corn, *Maize*; tomatoes, *Solanum lycopersicum*; beans, *Fabaceae;* potatoes, *Solanum tuberosum*. I think the bears would approve. Not of the shirt or the book—they don't do shirts or books in the wild. But they'd like to eat the veggies as I do. While constructing the book, I refused to include vegetables I don't like—so you won't find any nasty Brussels sprouts, *Brassica oleracea,* on my pages.

Every summer I grow a few herbs outside my kitchen door, but I do most of my foraging at the grocery store. Like the nearby bears, I know where to find wild berries—tiny strawberries, *Fragaria vesca,* that hide in the grass; prickly blackberries, *Rubus fruticosus;* and raspberries, *Rubus idaeus,* in late June and early July. More often I find these goodies in the produce aisle or at the farmer's market. And while I'm happy to be a locavore and eat what's in season during the summer and early fall, I freely admit that those delicious berries still tempt me all winter too, despite their long trips to market.

If I had to feed myself from the wild, I would probably behave something like a black bear and consume a mostly vegetarian diet (skipping those nasty bees and larvae along with the Brussels sprouts). I'd ambush emerging dandelion, *Taraxacum officinale,* and cress, *Lepidium sativum,* lie in wait for my ostrich fern, *Matteuccia struthiopteris,* for its fiddleheads to pop out of the rich damp soil. I'd add wild ramps, *Allium tricoccum,* to my culinary concoctions for zest and flavor. If pressed and very hungry, I might also harvest some of that infamous skunk cabbage, which supposedly tastes much better than it smells. But not too much, as it contains calcium oxalate crystals, which can cause a burning sensation in the mouth.

I can recognize several varieties of nuts, and acorns can be eaten if one first boils them to leach away the bitter-tasting tannin. If I had a reliable expert along, I'd happily hunt for wild mushrooms as well.

Again, like the bears, I could manage fish. As a child, I caught small sunnies, *Lepomis,* from a nearby creek and tossed them back. As an adult, I've caught real fish, sort of. On a fishing charter in Lake Michigan, I actually pulled in lake salmon and lake trout, *Salvelinus namaycush*—good sized ones. Of course the boat captain did most of the real work. He provided all equipment, including Dramamine, used his radar to find the fish, attached the hooks and lures, and set the poles in place. Once we pulled in our fish, he also kindly unhooked them, and then back on shore he cleaned and scaled them, and took some off for smoking. Back at the house, I watched as my now-deceased father-in-law destroyed an electric knife, trying to hack one of those large salmon into steaks. But in a small way, I have helped to catch fish that I've then eaten. I could learn the entire process if I needed to; I'm not squeamish.

In fact, when I was a teenager, I cooked and ate wild-found protein. My younger cousin Mark once challenged me to go out shooting frogs. To preserve my place as top chick in the family pecking order, I had to say yes. Once he'd shot the frog, I suggested dissecting it as I'd done in bio lab, and then showed off with his pocketknife. Once we'd checked out the various organs, I had the brilliant notion that we could cook and eat the frog legs. Which we did, shocking all of our parents, and even ourselves, once the warming legs began to dance in the hot butter.

☆

Afterwards, I had one regret—I wished we'd shot more frogs. They were delicious and I've eaten them since in restaurants. But when I say we, it is an error. *My cousin* shot the frog. I've never shot any live thing. I don't know if I could.

I have handled a rifle though. Once. Age sixteen. My high school had a rifle range and a rifle team. All boys, very cute boys. My friends and I hung around with them for a couple of months and one afternoon, they sneaked us down into the range and set us up with loaded rifles and paper targets.

From my adult perspective, the number of ways this was wrong heads toward infinity: no adults present; no firearms training; no safety information; no protective gear; and on and on. But as a young girl with a rifle in her hands and a good-looking boy standing close and showing me how to aim, it was amazing. Even more so when I hit the target near the center—good eyes and steady hands. So if I knew how to use a rifle, properly and safely, I might actually be able to bring home dinner.

The problem is not eyes or hands, it's my heart. I've watched a crow, *Corvus brachyrhynchos,* take out a fledgling robin as the parent birds scolded and chased. I've seen a red tail swoop down and return to the sky with five feet of wriggling blacksnake, *Coluber constrictor,* in his beak. I've stood motionless as a heron gigged for fish and frogs. I know how life and death sit next to each other on this bench of earth and yet each time I witness a natural violence, I feel saddened.

When I see animals sprawled by the side of the highway, I always wonder about their families—if it's a fawn, I wonder about the doe and if she's grieving. If it's a full-grown raccoon, I worry about the kits—what will they do without a mother? I worry less about opossums, *Didelphimorphia,* because I think they're ugly and creepy looking, sort of like oversized whitish rats. And skunks, forget it. I just hope they get hit far, far from my house and yard. Phew!

I haven't eaten road kill, though I know some folks do if they find it when fresh or if they are the driver who connects with the animal. And bears do too; if these omnivores happen to be in the right place at the right time they will help themselves. (Obviously the dead critter was in the wrong place . . .)

While I usually swerve to avoid hitting anything, I might be able to manage harvesting some of the wild turkeys that parade along the edge of the wetland. I think this is possible partly because I already eat turkey and partly because they too are on the ugly side. If I were after a turkey, I'd prefer a snare or a net to a gun though.

If hungry enough, I might also manage to dig up fresh snapping turtle eggs and find a way to eat them. And why not? It's not that big a stretch from frog to turtle. And there are lots of turtles in the area—they're not endangered. When the baby turtles emerge from their nests in early September, birds of all sizes gather to feast, allowing only a few to make it to the creek in safety. The turtle hatchlings look like nothing more than Oreo cookies for the birds. So my egg predation wouldn't make a significant difference in the species' survival.

Many folks in my father's family were hunters so I'm familiar with the concept of eating rabbits and squirrels; it's an acquired taste, but better than starving if that were my only option. As with the turkeys, I'd probably choose a snare rather than a gun, although once critters have fur, for me they start morphing from food source into cute.

My most serious challenge comes with bigger animals. In addition to the softness of heart, I also confess a lack of courage. Face down the ten-point buck that showed up in our front yard on the first day of hunting season? Not my style. I've had young deer in the woods step close enough to sniff at my hands, and besides that big guy has plenty of protection—hooves and that rack. I don't want to be anywhere in the vicinity when he lowers his head.

Worst of all is to imagine the bears. Even a young bear outweighs me and can outrun me. And more importantly, to my eye, they're too beautiful to destroy.

Is this illogical? Absolutely. I'm not naïve. I know where my food comes from. The beef at the butcher shop once mooed and grazed and walked about. The pork was once a cute, small piglet with a curly tail and little pointy ears. The chicken strutted about fluffing its feathers. I cook and eat all of the above. I just don't do my own dirty work. I don't kill them.

Could I? I don't know. I'd rather plant a big garden.

*Sharing bedroom space with a grizzly bear is not practical but sharing
wilderness space is. We must therefore, restrict human activity in spaces where
threatened or endangered species live. We must stay out of their bedroom.*

—Bob McMeans

☆

hide and seek

I FEEL LIKE Goldilocks. I have three bears, Mama and two cubs.
They show themselves to my neighbors, leave paw prints, drop scat,
but keep their faces hidden from me. Others in our family are playing hide-and-seek with bears this summer too.

"You're not the only ones with a bear story," my California daughter tells me on the phone. "We went on a camping trip into the Sequoia
National Park. They have tons of bears there, so we stored our food
and supplies in a bear-box. They're these sturdy, metal chests with
complicated locks and the park provides them at all the campsites.
Otherwise, the bears will break into your car."

In the middle of the night, her husband wakes her in the tent. He
hears a bear. "Go back to sleep," she says. "It's not a bear. You're worrying about nothing and waking me up." But next morning, they find
large paw prints on their bear-box.

The next report comes from my mother-in-law in the Colorado
Rockies. She too sleeps through the excitement. As on our property,
a large black bear breaks into her garage. Her garage, however, offers
much more reward for the hungry invader than our cottage—she has
a large, full, chest-type freezer. The bear enters at night, rips open the
freezer lid and begins looting. He munches as he flings treasures out

the door—ice cream cartons, various entrees, an entire beef tenderloin, frozen vegetables, breads, cookies. But this is inefficient—like carrying a small basket at the grocery store when you really need the extra-large cart.

Granny's bear is an innovator. He tries to drag the entire freezer out the narrow door he's broken into, crashing it into her car in the process and making a dent. Because he works at night, nobody spots him during his spree—but he's not exactly a stranger. Other houses up and down the road have been looted earlier in the summer. This bear is house-savvy.

It turns out he's also trap savvy, for when the Colorado Department of Wildlife sets up a large steel cage of a live bear trap and baits it with fruits, canned salmon and marshmallows nothing happens—no bear. The bait simply sits in the Colorado sunshine and the magpies, *Pica pica,* make pigs of themselves.

Meanwhile, Granny has to take her car to the body shop to the tune of $1,700. She buys a new freezer and refills it. A bear re-enters the yard several times after the garage incident, but a dead-bolt on the door seems to be keeping it outside. At this point, she sees bears as varmints and would be delighted to have the neighborhood nuisance removed—either relocated or put down. I can't blame her for this—she is, after all, an older woman living alone and vulnerable, as my neighbor Dina is, as I am much of the time. But I am still fascinated by bears. I continue to dig for more information, more facts, more photos on the web.

☆

A similar scenario could occur on our property. If we again spot our three bears and call the town police, they in turn will notify the wildlife police who will come and try to trap the bears and relocate them. It has happened before, at least I think so.

If you live in a city and a folkloric sort of story starts making the rounds, it soon earns the label, urban legend. What happens if a similar story circulates in a small mountain town? Does that become a rural legend? For me, such a title somehow lacks caché. In any case, several years ago, when we first moved to the country, such a story appeared.

Because of our proximity to New York City, we get summer and weekend visitors as well as numerous, part-time, vacation home-owners. We ourselves belong to that dubious category at present, until we move to the country full time when we become retirees. Better or worse category, hard to say.

Once we become voters, though, we won't be so obviously discriminated against. The town is a quintessential New England town—the village that appeared on so many of Norman Rockwell's *Saturday Evening Post* covers. They have a town meeting as part of the governing structure, but at these meetings, the real residents sit in chairs on the floor. Part-timers like ourselves are relegated to the bleachers and can observe but not participate.

It happened that one of these part-timers, a celebrity and bird lover, lived by the town pond. And yes, he'd heard the cautions about putting out seed before December, when the bears would be in hibernation. But this guy was smart—he had a system. Instead of hanging the feeder from a tree branch near the ground or nailing it to a post, he hung it from a second floor window—too far off the ground for a bear to reach. So far, so good.

Birds don't have great table manners, however. They dish seeds around with their beaks and spill large quantities—large enough to attract a bear. This particular feeder dangled above a room-sized air conditioner, a window unit. One evening while the homeowner was out, a mother bear with cub sniffed out the seed and came to munch. The air conditioner was located up off the ground, but not too far up, so Mama climbed atop the unit, which immediately crashed to the ground.

The resulting open space was too much for the cub—it darted inside and began racing around and around in the bedroom. The mother bear was too large to fit through the hole and the cub was having too much fun to return to Mama. The homeowner arrived home to find a small bear tearing up the bedroom and a furious sow raging outside the window. He called for assistance.

While this may be a rural legend, it probably contains a core of truth, because that same summer, the local paper reported that two bears, a mother and cub, had to be put down. They were breaking and entering in properties by the town pond.

☆

If my bears should appear while the lawn guy is working our story will be different but the ending will be equally final.

"What then?" I ask him on his next visit. "If you do what needs to be done, what happens afterward? Will you get in trouble?" I realize I am speaking in code. I can't quite make my mouth shape the words, *if you kill my bears* . . .

"No trouble, although I would have to report it to the wildlife people. And I'd need to explain the circumstances, since it's not bear season. Then I'd have to haul them in for checking and processing within forty-eight hours."

Them. He says *them.* So he would take out the cubs too. I should have expected it. He is too wise a woodsman to leave such young animals alone in the woods, vulnerable without their mother. He will offer them the clean, quick, painless death rather than the slow misery of injury or starvation. I switch mental channels to sort out the rest of what he's saying. "Checking? Processing?"

"Yeah. The wildlife guys have official checking stations where a biologist weighs the bear and removes a tooth for aging," he explains.

Aging would not be a challenge with the cubs, this year's batch.

"And then?" I have to ask.

"Processing. It's like the butcher shop. I belong to the Sportsman's Club. We have a wild banquet twice a year, so they'll receive the meat and freeze it, since it's out of season. All perfectly legal."

"Right." It all makes sense and I'm glad my friend won't get in trouble, but it leaves my stomach twitching. If I'm to believe reported comments from the famous hunter, Teddy Roosevelt, young bear tastes like wild boar. If I'm to believe my husband, bear chili tastes heavy and gamey. In either case, I'm not attending that tasting. I don't say the words aloud, but in my mind they shout.

Hide, bears. Hide.

If more of us valued food and cheer and song above hoarded gold, it would be a merrier world . . .

—J. R. R. Tolkien

playing with food

I'VE WATCHED A cat toy with a mouse. She pounces, grabs it in her mouth then drops it. The mouse runs but she swats, then pounces and grabs again. Clearly the cat is not hungry at the moment—the chase is all-important—her afternoon's entertainment. If I liked mice better, I might feel some sympathy for the poor little guy but I don't. I just want it to be over. I want the cat to win and the mouse to be out of sight, out of my living quarters, dead, gone and away.

In a different way, cartoon pals Yogi Bear and Boo Boo enjoy playing with food, but their play consists of outsmarting the nearby humans. Yogi is, after all, smarter than the average bear. He steals the pic-a-nic baskets. In real life, this translates as bear wisdom—maximizing food intake, upping the calories per hour.

☆

This summer I can't play with my own food. The kitchen is under construction. It is currently an empty room, nicely walled-in, with pipes poking up from the floor and wires protruding from various ceiling and wall openings. Most of the contractor's work is done and we're waiting for the cabinetmaker to complete the kitchen cabinets and install them so we can move on to appliances and flooring.

I've been hoping to find a finished kitchen when we arrive on Memorial Day weekend, but it looks more like we'll settle back in closer to July Fourth. I move the fridge and microwave onto the sun porch and stock up on large quantities of paper and plastic ware. I'll have a very Yogi Bear and Boo Boo sort of month, an ongoing pic-a-nic but I really won't be able to cook. And that bothers me.

I don't steal picnic baskets or torment mice, but I like to play with my food. I'm the sort of cook who opens the fridge and checks out the contents. What do we have, and how might these various in-gredients combine to make something new and interesting? Except when baking, I'm not a recipe follower. I do read recipes, and when one looks interesting, I use it as a starting point and adapt it to family tastes, what's in season, what's in the house. I also enjoy hopping onto various cooking websites to see what other folks have done with some of the ingredients I happen to have at the moment.

☆

From what I've seen of cooks, it's often an either/or situation. People seem to either follow recipes or improvise. My traditionalist daughter seeks out recipes and follows them, while her more experimental younger sister invents. One friend is an extremely conservative recipe guy—he carries a copy of a new recipe to the grocery store and buys precisely what is required in precisely the quantities described. In the kitchen he diligently completes each step exactly as written.

"That makes sense, for the first time you make something," I say, trying to sound generous and affirming. "But what happens after-ward? Do you change anything the next time you make that dish?"

"Oh, no. Not at all. Maybe after I've made it four or five times, I might change one ingredient—but generally I don't change it at all."

This blows me away. I'm trying hard to imagine making the same thing four or five times without changing it and can't. But then I look at him closely—he's perfectly groomed, coordinated, polished. I'm more tossed together, of the moment, in both attire and cuisine. In the kitchen or the closet, sometimes I pull it off and sometimes I don't. But I love the experimentation. I'm guessing that all has to do with the rebellious side of my nature—why follow the rules and do as others expect, when you can just play?

☆

For the coming weeks, I'll be playing with frozen and microwave meals, and with the various local takeout options. Yawn. So boring and predicable. I can't even boil pasta, one of the staples of my eclectic style of cooking.

That very predictability was essential to me as a child, however. I was the quintessential picky eater. When my parents went to a restaurant, they'd order me a tomato juice, a couple of lemon slices to chew on, and some saltines. I would happily eat those items. But if they ordered even a simple peanut butter and jelly sandwich, I'd balk. The cook used the wrong kind of jelly. If they ordered me a bowl of tomato soup, a home favorite, I'd turn up my nose if the kitchen prepared it with milk instead of water. My poor mother worried that I'd never eat properly. But it was partly her fault. She was an excellent traditional cook and baker. Was I to blame if other people's food didn't taste as good as hers? Of course not. And life can be unfair, for as it turned out, my daughters were not picky eaters, so no hints of maternal revenge ever surfaced in that area.

As I grew older, my tastes changed and so did the eating options for most Americans. Canned fruits and veggies gave way to frozen ones, and then, with increasing speeds of transport, fresh foods became available from many different climates during most of the year. All this food, just waiting for a young cook to play with. This was progress. Of course it happened in the bad old days, before we counted up the energy costs of shipping strawberries from California or South America in mid-winter. Before we had a locavore, slow-food ethic.

So of course I took it on, bought all those fresh foods and discovered a wider palate. Hot and spicy. Interesting mixtures of meats and vegetables, prepared quickly, no overcooking. New grains and varieties of rice, *Oryza*, barley, *Hordeum vulgare,* couscous (from durum wheat, *Triticum).*

Ironically I now find it frustrating to cook for or go to a restaurant with my mother. She's the picky one. Most ethnic cooking is off her list. Even traditional cooking must be done the right way—her way. *These green beans weren't cooked long enough. This sauce is too spicy. I only like pepperoni on my pizza.* As I watch her push food around on her plate, a poor imitation of really eating, I can feel the memory in my muscles. I did the same exact thing as a small child. If I spread out those detestable peas, wouldn't it look like I'd eaten some? Wouldn't the grownups please, please release me from the table? No, they wouldn't. Didn't.

The thing is, my mother hasn't changed. She's still the same traditional cook and eater from long ago, although living in a retirement community, she's finally getting a well-earned rest from all the daily kitchen duty. She now only cooks once in a while, and still prepares her standards from long ago. And they still taste fine, if to my tongue somewhat bland. This isn't her fault. I'm the one who's changed, who's embraced new tastes and flavors and textures. So it's rather unfair of me to be critical. But then aren't offspring always critical of their parents? Doesn't it come with the generational territory? My daughters certainly give me plenty of feedback.

This summer, however, I'm the one released from kitchen duty, even when we have guests. I'm doomed to endure the endless picnic, to which Yogi and Boo Boo would love to be invited. While it gets a little repetitive, it's not all bad. I have more time with my guests when I don't have to worry about three squares a day times eight people.

"Help yourself," I say. "The food's in the fridge." Cleanup is a breeze—get out the trash bags. So it's a vacation for me. And when my kitchen is finally done, I know I'll be ready to chop and peel and slice and sauté again. But in the meantime I won't go hungry. I just won't get to play with my food.

☆

What about bears though? The ones in my backyard, not the ones in the Saturday morning cartoons. Sure, they'd happily help themselves to my picnics if I set them out on the lawn. But I won't do that. I may be occasionally rebellious but I'm not stupid.

Instead I wonder about their food habits—how do they learn to eat the proper foods? Is it simply scent—like the way the smell of Toll House cookies baking sets me to salivating—or is there learning involved?

For the first year of life, cubs are nursed by their mothers, but they also browse and forage with her. Perhaps in that way she helps to train their noses and taste buds. *Here, eat this. Willow (Salix) shoots are good for you . . .* In fact they are—the bark contains acetylsalicylic acid, aspirin, which might help a bear deal with any leftover aches and pains while emerging from hibernation in the spring. Or, *Drink up, drink up, the weather is getting colder. If you don't drink now, you'll be thirsty later . . .* Again, a strategy mature bears use in the fall to prepare for hibernation. Perhaps Mama even teaches her cubs to look out for the occasional human food source like our cottage or our dumpster.

I wonder if these little bears complain about the new tastes and textures, about the strange lumpy food. I could imagine that they might only want milk and sweet berries and honey. That they'd stick out their bottom lips and pout like I did. That they'd grow critical of Mama Bear's diet choices or find the spaghetti sauce in my garbage can too spicy.

By the second spring, when new plant growth is leafing out, when nests of insects contain fat grubs, Mama Bear weans her cubs and they eat on their own. Having watched a video of a young cub smashing a rotten log to get at a nest of ant larvae, I find answers to some of my questions. Bears don't worry much about recipes or food preparation. If it's in season, it's on the menu. They aren't picky or critical and they don't play with their food. They simply eat it.

Hunger is all.

*. . . With a big brown furry-down up to my head, I'd sleep all
the winter in a big fur bed.*

— A. Milne

snow bears

A FRIEND OF mine suffers from Seasonal Affective Disorder. When
the days grow shorter and the sunlight is less direct she experiences
symptoms of depression—*the winter blues.* Included in this condition:
a drop in energy; too much sleep; general malaise. In the far north—
Scandinavia, Iceland, Lapland, Siberia—these symptoms occur with
greater frequency than in more southerly latitudes. Treatments include
exposing the body to more light, through natural sunlight (taking
daily outdoor walks) and adding bright, white, full-spectrum artificial light to the interior environment. Additionally, supplements of
vitamin D and the hormone melatonin may be used to help moder-
ate the body's response to the decrease in light.

While I find that my daily rhythms do change with the seasons, I
don't grow sluggish or depressed in the winter—I enjoy it if dressed
for the weather. So I don't spend my winters in Florida, as it turns
out. My husband and I traveled there in February once, not long ago,
and found it crowded and unnaturally hot. We're not Snow Birds by
disposition—we like the full array of four seasons and look forward
to the day when we will live in New England year round. Purists in the
area actually claim that the Berkshires have not four but eight distinct
seasons. Sounds great.

Okay, I might not enjoy mud season, late March and early April. For those weeks, I might be persuaded to visit Tuscany or Spain, but the rest of the year the Berkshires offer beauty and variety out every window. And I'm not a hibernator—inside peering out—I'm out enjoying the seasons, whether trekking on snowshoes or cross-country skis, paddling in a kayak or climbing a slope in hiking boots.

My bears do hibernate—perhaps the ultimate example of intense winter sleep. In late summer and early fall, in preparation, they put on pounds of body fat to sustain them for the months of fasting. In this stage, called hyperphagia, they increase their intake from about 8,000 calories per day to 15,000–20,000 calories. They gorge themselves with food and drink large quantities of water to help them process the food and to rid their bodies of wastes.

As the weather cools, they undergo a fall transition. They eat less but continue to drink to purge wastes. They grow lethargic and sleep most of the time and their heart rates begin to slow.

From November through April they den up and undergo the most dramatic physiological changes. The heart rate drops from a normal sleeping rate of 40–50 beats per minute to a hibernation rate of 8–20 beats per minute. Their oxygen consumption also drops, so that a bear in deep hibernation may need to breathe only once every 45 seconds. Interestingly, unlike some other hibernating animals, their body temperatures do not drop.

They neither eat nor eliminate during this dormant time and nitrogen wastes are recycled through the body as proteins, which helps prevent muscle loss. Occasionally, when the weather warms, during a January thaw for example, a bear will leave the den briefly, eat a bit of snow, wander about as if confused, then return to hibernation.

Females rouse to give birth in February and suckle their cubs until the snow melts; their high body temperatures help warm the new cubs who are born about eight inches long, less than a pound in weight, and covered with fine, soft grey hair. The cubs operate at full metabolism from birth, and so nurse extensively to fuel themselves. When the bears emerge from winter dens, the adults wander about for two to three weeks in a stage of walking hibernation. They begin to eat and drink, but not in large quantities, and as more and more spring food sources appear, they gradually re-acclimate their metabolisms to an active summer level.

☆

Orpheus traveled into the underworld in search of his beloved, Eurydice. His great tragedy was that he didn't obey instructions—he looked back, unwilling to trust that she would follow him into the land of the living. He paid the price—he could return to the world, but Eurydice would remain behind, forever lost to him.

Like Orpheus, bears have been seen by many cultures as travelers between two worlds—between the living and the dead. Their suspended state during hibernation has fascinated people, both ancient and modern. In Native American mythology, the bear is a frequent totem or spirit animal. His medicine—his essential spirit—is his ability to enter a deep meditative state and return, rejuvenated and reborn. This cycle of contemplation and rebirth can be experienced symbolically, through a spirit journey, which might include time spent in deep meditation in a kiva or sweat lodge.

The bear's journey does not, in fact, parallel Orpheus' tragedy, for when the bear returns he returns to life—to feast and to reproduce—not to mourn. Perhaps bear is more like Persephone, who enters the underworld land of Demeter, her mother, for half the year and returns with the advent of spring, of warmth, of growth. Her return, like that of bear, is cause for celebration. The earth will be fruitful once more.

☆

It occurs to me to wonder where the bears go when they want to hide. They don't literally travel deep underground, so where do they den? Dina points out a trail, a mashed down pathway through the underbrush and into the woods behind the cottage. Neither of us plans to follow it to confirm that it is the bear's homeward route, particularly not in high summer. Deep, frozen-over winter, maybe. With snowshoes on and a companion or two, I might brave it.

For now, I snoop on the internet, instead of in the woods. From what I have been able to discover, bears can be pretty casual about their dens. A hollowed out space—a brush pile, a large fallen tree, a jumble of rocks, a mountain laurel thicket, *Kalmia latifolia,* a deserted manmade structure—anything that provides some minimal shelter will do. They have thick fur and heavy insulating body fat, so while they need shelter and some winter protection, they don't exactly need central heating.

Unlike the robins who nest in the rhododendron bushes next to the house, bears don't return to the same nest year after year, but settle in new ones. Another bear may settle into a previously used den, however. This makes sense when one considers the every-other-year nature of bear reproduction. In a year when a female is nursing a pair of good-sized yearling cubs, she'll need a larger space for her family, as compared to a year when she's pregnant and likely to give birth to tiny babies. An oversized and partially empty den will not stay as warm as a smaller enclosure. And unlike mine, bears' nesting impulses don't run to paint and fabric, to auctions and yard sales. Instead they might line the den with leaves or grasses.

Regardless of size or construction materials, once a mother bear settles, she's likely to sleep with her back to the opening and her body curled inward, shielding herself from the cold with the thick fur on her back and protecting her face and her babies from the cold. She will also pay attention to the buildup of water in the den. As the weather warms and the snow melts (that wretched mud season again), water collecting in the den can endanger newborn cubs. They can chill from the wetness or even drown, so the mother may add branches or extra bedding materials to keep her brood high and dry.

All of this makes me wonder about our decaying outbuilding tucked away in the underbrush. If I were Mama Bear, I'd certainly appreciate four walls and half a roof. A wooden floor. No serious snowmelt. I'm not using that building, but I wonder if she is—I have my house, Dina has hers, and the bear may have one too. I like the symmetry. Maybe I will take a peek when the snow falls.

☆

This year I'm making warm wooly slippers for all the children in our family. If I make a mistake in my knitting, painful as it can be, I can pull out rows of errant stitches or even the whole piece, and roll the yarn back onto the ball in order to start again. All these bear thoughts, though, can't be so easily unpicked. Once dark notions intrude, they persist, like knots and tangles in my mind.

Hard as I try, I can't forget that my friend the lawn guy may have my bears in his rifle sights one day. I must work hard to erase from my mind the vision of roast bear. And even if my friend doesn't remove the bears, they are, as we are, mortal creatures. Like it or not, one day they will die as one day we will die.

Absent human interference, hunting or trapping, black bears live for eighteen to twenty years in the wild. What happens when the life ends? Do they go off deep into the woods and hide? It would be quite a shock to go for a hike and just stumble on a bear carcass. But the scavengers and predators will do their work and feed on the remains. The coyotes, the American crows, and the maggots (the larvae of flies, *Diptera* will eventually erase the presence of even a huge old bear, except for small tufts of black fur, sharp fragments of white bone.

And then what? Will a new lady bear come to take the place of the old? Will the territory be claimed once again, perhaps by a daughter or granddaughter bear?

Heavy thoughts, but when I do the math, my mood lightens. We've only lived on this land for ten years. My bear wasn't necessarily an old lady when we arrived, so perhaps she has a number of good years left. More springs to wake. More cubs to raise. More skunk cabbage to eat. I hope so.

Wherever you are, bears. Hide. Hide.

☆

. . . the bear went over the mountain, to see what he could see . . .

—Traditional Tune

☆

on bear mountain

WE CROSS FROM Pennsylvania into New York and a sudden tension enters my shoulders; it feels more nervous than excited. Then I realize that this August a question mark awaits at journey's end. How much permanent damage from the June windstorm? We've received bills from the tree removal guys so the trunks, limbs and branches will be gone. But we don't know what remains behind, or how wrecked my gardens will be. I am a ferocious digger in the dirt—I take personally any assault on my landscape.

When we cross over from New York into Massachusetts, a short half hour from home, I'm bouncing in my seat, barely able to stay in the car. When we reach the house, I tear open the door and rush toward the back garden, my favorite.

Oddly, in early summer, I'd noted aloud that the garden had an overgrown feel—the red twig dogwood, *Cornus sericea*, especially. I'd need to do some serious pruning. Perhaps my remarks were seriously listened to, for broken branches lie everywhere and the root ball of the huge white pine still stands upright, pointing toward the sky. Mother Nature has pruned quite severely. As I look closely at the garden, however, I notice that most of the shrubs and bushes have new green leaves sprouting from their bases.

Three days, much sweat, and dozens of trips to the compost pile later, everyone looks young and healthy again. My arm and leg muscles sing with the work. We ask about the bears, but late summer has been quiet. No sightings. Our neighbor believes that once the Dumpster got hauled away, the bears lost interest in the property. She may be right. For her sake and the bears', I hope so.

And of course they hauled the Dumpster away because the kitchen renovation is finally complete and we can cook and eat again. The bears may not be feasting here, but we are.

☆

The weather beams down, sunny and glorious all week, so once we tidy the storm damage we plan some day hikes. My husband has two in particular that he wants to try—a creek trail with several dramatic waterfalls and Bear Mountain, the mountain with the highest summit in nearby Connecticut.

We'd tried the creek trail a couple of years earlier, but were unable to cross the first of several fords because of high water. Again this year, we find too much water. The previous week's rains have made the creek too deep and the fords too dangerous. So we treat the mile-long start of the creek hike as a warm-up for Bear Mountain.

Late the next morning we check the guidebook briefly before tucking it into our pack. "Lunch?" I ask.

"It sounds like a short enough hike," he says. "And we're getting a late start. Let's not waste time packing a lunch. I'll grab water bottles and apples."

It takes half an hour of winding along back roads to reach the trailhead. The day is warm, humid, and the hike steep. The late start means we must hike with the sun high overhead. We climb and climb and it seems like we're working harder, climbing longer than the book said we should. Underfoot, the soft, forgiving forest detritus gives way to granite outcroppings, exposed roots, small spills of water to cross.

I feel the heat, the fatigue, and grumble about it. My heart pounds and I get winded, soaked with sweat that, in the humidity, doesn't evaporate to cool me. I stop often, drink a lot of my water. A quick check of the guidebook brings bad news.

"We've misread the trail descriptions," he says. "That elevation gain and two mile, steep, uphill hike only gets us to the junction with the Appalachian Trail."

"Great," I reply. "How much farther."

"Another mile of steep hiking to the summit at 2 3 2 3 feet."

"You're kidding, right?" But he's not. The three and a half to four hour round trip now looks like five to six hours.

My husband is still game, but I go on strike. I'm hot, hungry, winded, sore and very grumpy. If I'd known the hike would be so long, I'd have packed a good trail lunch and more water. I'd have insisted we leave earlier while morning coolness still clung to the trail. I mention these facts more than once. An unkind person might use the word nagging.

"Let's just get to Riga Junction," he urges.

I agree, but grudgingly. Once there, I plant myself on a rock. "You go ahead. Climb to the top. I'll wait here. I'm not going any farther."

He persuades me. He's made this trip before and knows that the top is spectacular. And we're so close.

I'm not sure I believe him—spectacular, sure, but close? I trudge along anyway and as often happens, the nearer we should be getting, the more distant the summit appears. Finally, I just stop. "I've had it. I'm not going any farther. I'll come back in the fall on a cool day when we have lunch."

Good sport that he is, he sets off by himself to scout it out. He returns in less than five minutes. "I've been to the summit and back. You can do it. We'll take it slow."

This is a gentlemanly sort of hiker—one who knows that to hike happily with a much shorter woman is to let her set the pace. So, reluctantly, I step up and up and up.

Finally, an enormous stone pyramid appears—built in 1885 of 350 tons of stone, by a stonemason, Robbins Battell, and restored twice since. I climb to the top on jittery legs and sit where I can see a panorama—endless sky above, a pair of lakes below, Massachusetts to the north, the Catskills and New York to the west. Spectacular.

I devour my one small apple as greedily as a bear might. Other hikers enjoy the summit with us, and they've brought tons of food. Which they consume completely. I find myself staring, practically drooling, as they empty bags of chips, packets of cheese, but this doesn't provoke the sharing impulse in the least. Not one chip, not a crumb of cheese. I wonder about this as the large group is mostly teenagers with some adults along to supervise. Haven't these adults taught the kids that sharing is a virtue? Obviously not—instead they obey another dictum of the woods—carry in, carry out. Next time, next time . . . more food.

We also meet a young guy in a full pack whom I identify correctly as a thru-hiker on the Appalachian Trail. He began in Maine, hiking since early summer, and is heading south toward Georgia. He hopes to reach trail's end by Thanksgiving. Just hearing the word makes me think turkey, stuffing, a feast. My stomach growls.

Seeing him so well outfitted reminds me of my own early adulthood when I backpacked every other weekend in the White Mountains of New Hampshire. My younger self would be ashamed of me today—both the whining and complaining, and the poor preparation. Next time, next time . . . more planning, more spirit, more spunk.

We head down, and again I lead the way. My husband is the better uphill hiker while I'm more surefooted going down. It feels good to descend, to use different muscles, to cool off, to not get winded. This bear of a mountain has challenged me as wilderness often does. I must learn not to underestimate bears of any sort.

☆

I also must not underestimate the eating imperative, the first law of the wild—eat, eat, and then eat some more. We live in a land of plenty —a country rich with food sources. We have huge mega-supermarkets and small ethnic groceries. Bagel shops and pizza shops. Fast food and slow food and take-out. In other parts of the world people struggle daily to eat, but here in the United States, many people have forgotten the essential nature of this our most primary need: to nourish ourselves.

I plead guilty to such forgetting. I've never gone truly hungry in my life. This morning, as we prepared for the hike in a new, shiny kitchen dedicated to cooking fine meals, I took a casual attitude toward food. Lunch? Not a big deal. This afternoon, I paid for my disregard in discomfort—in fatigue and a growling belly.

My bear would not be so foolish. She eats to live, but in the most primitive, essential sense, she also lives to eat, as we all do. This drive directs her every life pattern. The size of her territory and her unwillingness to share the range means more food, enough food, to sustain her. Hibernation means she will not have to struggle to eat when food sources grow scarce, but rather will emerge to feast when the new plants sport spring foliage. Her long lactation means that her offspring will grow healthy and strong enough to survive on their own. Her acute sense of smell and long memory give her predictable feasting grounds, year after year. Her dietary flexibility, both plants and animals, varying by the season provides a rich, diverse menu. Given a choice, fighting with other creatures burns calories while eating adds them. She'll almost always choose to eat. I could learn a lot from this bear I've been watching.

☆

At day's end, after a shower, we feast on an incredible restaurant dinner—pasta, that unbeatable comfort food, topped with an exquisite sauce. Later, when I recheck the climb on the internet, I find myself agreeing with the guide: . . . *the hikes up to Bear Mountain are*

tough ones for the average day-hiker but you don't have to be in world class
shape to attempt it. With a little patience, plenty of water and snacks, and
determination, the rewards far outweigh the strains of climbing up the tallest
peak in Connecticut. And you'll be proud and happy you did!

Proud and happy? I'm getting there. I completely agree about the water and snacks. Also the determination—my husband's, not mine, prevailed.

And the toughness? Absolutely. A bear, is a bear, is a bear, after all. Even when it happens to be a mountain.

surrounded

THE BEARS ARE coming after me.

A picture arrives in my in-box titled *Change of Plan for Hunting Season*. A large black bear sits up high in a hunter's stand in a clump of Eastern hemlocks, *Tsuga canadensis*. The same friend sends another attachment two days later, a series of Power Point slides showing a family that has raised a grizzly, *Ursus arctos horribilis*, from a cub and it is now living as a member of the family. Toilet trained. Joining Thanksgiving Dinner. I wonder if it gets its own turkey. That name, though. *Horribilis*. It makes me stop and think.

Another friend brings me a tourist booklet from eastern Pennsylvania with a large black bear on the cover. I have shared a couple of my essays with writer friends and now am feeling surrounded.

As I've already done a bear inventory in the Massachusetts house, I feel obliged to tramp upstairs and conduct one here in Pittsburgh too. Surely most of the bears have migrated from this urban house to the country; the terrain is so much friendlier to bears there in the wilds.

Nope. I count twenty bears, large and small, well-dressed, undressed, and totally unfashionable, living happily among the other stuffed critters on the third floor. One more sits in a child-sized rocker in the dining room and another hides in the finished basement room wearing reindeer antlers and sneaking peeks at movies and football games. Twenty-two bears in all and I am responsible for none of them. They were all gifts for my daughters when they were small. The largest house bear stands taller than a year-old child. The smallest, a three-inch, heavy glass bear in cobalt blue, insists on coming down with me to sit on my computer and supervise while I write these essays. Somebody has to act as fact-checker.

I can't escape. Just when I think I've completed my inventory, I travel to central Pennsylvania for a three-day writer-in-residence job at a community college. Their mascot, the black bear. When the college president hears of my bear fixation, he gives me a gift from the bookstore, a small, soft black teddy bear wearing a college sweater. Bears begin appearing on birthday cards and my husband gives me a set of bear ears with matching bow tie.

Bears thrive at the grocery store too, Gummy Bears, Teddy Grahams, Bear Creek Soup Mix, honey sold in bear-shaped jars. Strange, twisted bears try to sell me Charmin Toilet Tissue. No thank you. Bears don't use toilet tissue. For heaven's sake, there's a Bear Brand knitting yarn.

And the songs. Many of them are for kids—"Winnie the Pooh," "Lions and Tigers and Bears, oh my!" "Teddy Bears' Picnic," some Gummy Bear song, "Teddy Bear, Teddy Bear Turn Around."

I happen to like "The Parade of the Teddy Bears." Maybe it's the march tempo. My husband plays it on the piano and I sing it loudly every Christmas, even when nobody is listening.

"The Bear Went Over the Mountain" seems dirty to me, somehow. I've always felt that if I only knew *all* the lyrics, I'd catch on to the joke. And that Davy Crockett. He "killed him a b'ar when he was only three." What a guy. Even Elvis got into the act. He wanted to be my teddy bear. Right. When he was the sexiest young guy alive and I was a geeky, skinny little kid. And now there's even a rock band called Grizzly Bear.

☆

We live in a bear-infested world. And it's confusing. Smokey the Bear, for instance. When a large, imposing creature tells you that you have power, you tend to believe him. Especially if you're a small, unimposing child. I grew up thinking of Smokey the Bear as my friend; he is recognized by most adults and by three-fourths of all the children in the United States. The mascot of the United States Forest Service, he was created in 1944 to educate the public about the danger of forest fires; it was one of the most successful advertising campaigns ever developed.

During World War Two, when most able-bodied men, including my dad, were off fighting in Europe, North Africa, or the Pacific, women, older men, and teenagers provided labor on farms and in factories that supported the war effort. With so many young men gone, few of the people who remained at home were skilled enough or available to fight forest fires. The West Coast was particularly vulnerable due to the hot, dry climate in many areas. And what the Forest Service saw as a danger, the Japanese viewed as a weapon.

In 1942, using submarines, the Japanese launched incendiary bombs in an unsuccessful attempt to set Oregon's coastal forests afire. Later, in 1944 and 1945, nine thousand fire balloons were set adrift from Japan into the jet stream loaded with similar bombs. About ten percent floated clear across the Pacific and made it to the United States. One exploded near Bly, Oregon, killing five children and their teacher who had found the balloon and were investigating it.

Also in 1942, Walt Disney released the movie *Bambi,* which features a ferocious forest fire. For a year, the Bambi character was adopted by the Forest Service in fire prevention campaigns, but Disney owned Bambi; the Forest Service needed a permanent symbol. They chose a bear, named him Smokey and outfitted him with jeans, a hat borrowed from a Cavalry uniform, and a bucket to douse fires.

In 1950, an American black bear cub climbed a tree to escape a fire in the Capitan Mountains of New Mexico. He was rescued but his paws and back legs had been burned so at first he was called Hotfoot

Teddy. He was renamed Smokey, after the mascot, and took up residence in the National Zoo in Washington, D.C., where he became a celebrity. During his lifetime millions of people visited him and sent him letters—so many letters that he was given his own zip code: 20252. When he died in 1976, his obituary appeared in the *Washington Post,* the *Wall Street Journal* and hundreds of other newspapers.

These days, Smokey's message has been edited. It now resounds, in the deep, booming voice of actor Sam Eliot as, "Only you can prevent *wildfires.*" This change, from *forest* to *wild,* reflects a current ecological concern. If small accidental fires or controlled burns do not occur, large quantities of dry fuel will build up on the forest floor. When fire strikes under those conditions, it will be devastating and wide-ranging, killing everything in sight as in the Bambi movie. So Smokey's job is to help prevent accidental or intentional vandalism fires, as opposed to smaller, contained, healthy burns.

My botanist daughter worked for two years in the Santa Monica Mountains wearing a Smokey hat. Employed by the Forest Service, she and her colleagues surveyed large tracts of woodland, chaparral, and grassland. They inventoried all the plants growing within different sample sections of the mountains, so that when (not if) a burn came, plant experts could watch how various species would re-grow and repopulate the terrain. She also spent time interpreting the wilderness to visitors—like Smokey himself, an advocate of the natural world, wearing that familiar hat.

But she's not the only one. The more common sighting occurs when the siren roars to life and the flashing red and blue light looms up behind the car on the highway. State Troopers, State Police, the Highway Patrol, with different names in different states, these guys also wear the Smokey hat. Long distance truckers, in the early days of the citizens' band radio, began to call these officers Smokeys and later Bears. The nicknames have stuck.

behind bars

ZOOS ARE ALL about sex. It's not so much the *who does what to whom* that fills celebrity gossip columns, but off-site, zoos operate large, protected preserves where rare and endangered animals are safeguarded and bred. They also work to keep more plentiful and common captive animals from breeding on site. Seals, *Pinniped,* for example, whose pups may be orphaned in the wild and brought to a zoo to keep them alive—they are plentiful and don't need to reproduce in captivity so are often housed only with others of the same sex.

The Association of Zoos and Aquariums has a Species Survival Plan, which attempts to conserve endangered species that may not survive in the wild and prevent their extinction. The plan involves collaboration and coordination between various North American zoos so that a captive population will grow large and genetically diverse enough to continue to reproduce. In some cases, if the reproduction is successful, animals may be reintroduced back into the wild. Meanwhile, the captive animals benefit from superb veterinary medical care and extensive research. Large cats, elephants, and various small mammals and birds have been successfully bred in captivity.

Even though I know all this, I resist visiting. But the weather is changing. If I want to see the bears close up, I need to visit the zoo and soon. I invite a friend along to share lunch, the visit and lend moral support, knowing that her feelings about caged animals mirror mine. We choose a warm, blustery fall Wednesday when school is in session so most of the other visitors are families with preschool children.

The day is glorious and I'm tempted to change the itinerary, but don't. Red and yellow and gold leaves blaze along the hillsides. At the zoo, the breeze is stiff enough it tumbles bright leaves in the air like a giant kaleidoscope spinning fifty feet overhead.

As we begin the trek it feels as if someone has folded me in half and torn along the dotted line. The child side of me loves every animal she sees. And for a spell, at least, the grownup keeps her thoughts to herself. I surprise myself and forget to be critical. Instead, my fingers itch to touch the thick vibrant fur of the four tigers perched up on a rocky ledge. In fact, I want to pet all the large cats, but only in my fingers. My brain is more sensible.

And the children—in packs and strollers and wagons and on foot —my grandmother self admires them all. Some notice the large animals; some pay more attention to the common house sparrows, *Passeridae,* that flit down to the path. Most of the children chirp and call out with high-pitched, joyful voices.

My friend and I make our way directly to the bears and our first sighting is the polar bears, *Ursus maritimus.* The zoo has recently renovated the habitat so that the two polar bears swim in a large glassed-in pool and can climb the nearby rocky terrain. Visitors can observe from outdoors, but most amazing is the view from underneath, through the glass, where we watch one large bear swim, play with toys, gnaw on a bone. One mother sets a toddler up on a ledge so he can see better—she puts him closer to the big white bear. The little guy quite sensibly climbs down. He clearly doesn't want to be all that close.

For such a large animal, the bear swims easily, gracefully, and its fur ripples in the water as it glides. Beautiful to watch and more than a little odd to stand in such proximity. Like the toddler, I don't need to climb up on that ledge to get closer.

We move on to the black bears, the animals I've come to see. Their habitat, too, is mostly rocky terrain with several indentations, rimmed at the top with electric fencing. In one pseudo cave, a large animal is sleeping. Straw lines another cave, which looks to be the den of the smaller bear. When standing upright, she's about my height, maybe five feet, with glossy black fur and a well-shaped head.

Before visiting, I've wondered to myself, what do these captive animals do all day? In the wild, they'd spend the day eating and hunting food and eating, again and again. Here their food is provided, so they have no serious work. They have no purpose for their days.

The older bear is obviously sleeping the day away and I presume he's grown accustomed to the limited habitat. The younger one paces and rocks her head from side to side. She treads in endless clockwise circles to one of the indentations in the rock where it appears that the food is delivered. Then she turns and travels in a narrow radius, a loop of perhaps ten or fifteen square feet. This is disturbing. It reminds me of behavior of patients in mental hospitals or of incarcerated prisoners. In the wild this bear would own a territory of nine to ten square miles. Here she shares perhaps 300 square feet with another. Similarly, the polar bear would have an entire ocean in the wild, but is contained in a small pool here.

It feels very wrong. I can't help making comparisons between these animals and their constricted lives and what I see when I visit my parents in their retirement community. Like the bears, the elders there no longer have serious work. Many of my parents' friends have lost a sense of purpose for their days. They spend much of their time indoors, in small apartments. Some nap frequently. It seems a grim foreshadowing of what is to come.

Then I realize I need to get over myself, to stop anthropomorphizing. These bears seem content enough. The small one may be circling toward the food door because it's time for lunch. And if it weren't for this zoo, the bears wouldn't be alive at all. They'd have died as cubs in the wild.

☆

A boy of about eight stands with his parents next to us. He has questions about the bears and I have some answers. "No they aren't usually aggressive or ferocious. Yes, in the wild they'd be getting ready to hibernate soon. Yes, they have their babies in hibernation."

"Will they hibernate here? Does the zoo close in the winter? Do the fish freeze when water turns to ice?"

"I don't know," I tell him.

"Can we come back in the winter and see?" he asks his parents.

I ask the zookeepers. Yes, the zoo stays open all winter. And the fish and the bears do slow down in the cold, but they don't hibernate or die. Zookeepers feed the bears all winter, so while they sleep a lot, they still move about. For the fish, the real danger would be if the water stops moving—if it ices over and noxious gasses accumulate. So the zoo ponds include waterfalls and pumps, which oxygenate the waters, making them safe for fish.

Once I have a few answers, I want more. It turns out that the big reptiles, the crocodiles, *Crocodylidae,* and komodo dragons, *Varanus komodoensis,* are cold blooded; they must spend their winters indoors and out of view. But many of the mammals come and go in the weather. The gorillas, *Gorilla gorilla,* have pass-through doors and so go in and out at their own choice. And even the elephants, *Elephas* and *Loxodonta,* spend some winter days outside. Such a large body mass makes them tolerant of the cold—only their ears lose significant amounts of heat, so on cold days they sensibly hold their ears close to their heads. The zookeepers don't let the elephants go out when it's icy, though; they're heavy and could slip and injure a leg. Who but a zookeeper would know such interesting facts?

As often happens in my life, the children I see this afternoon teach me something important. Even the bars-and-cages side of zoos has great value. Some environmental advocates believe that if we are to protect this fragile planet, we must first learn to love its wild side. And we must start with the children. That boy with the questions, for example. The bears clearly fascinate him, so perhaps when he's older, he might care enough to want to help animals in the wild. Or the toddler who sensed the raw power of the great white polar bear. Perhaps he'll grow to respect the animals around him, wild and tame, great and small.

☆

As I'm leaving the bears, I see a sign. It informs me that captive lions differ from those of their species who live in the wild. They are healthier, better nourished and may live longer because they are protected from danger. Since they no longer hunt, their muscles are less well developed, and they are less speedy, but overall they live easier lives. They have adapted and make the most of their situation. And wild or captive, they protect their territory. Useful information. It helps me clarify, to balance the scales.

For the rest of the visit, I surrender to the child inside. After watching the bears for a long time we move on to other animals and observe the primates, those closest of cousins. Of all the creatures here, they seem the most acclimated to captivity. They are busy socializing, grooming each other. When a large silverback stands up and moves to a new spot in the grass, the younger gorillas step out of the way, much like the newest employee might when confronted by the CEO—the alpha animal of his pack. The smaller primates climb, scamper, swing, using those fascinating prehensile tails, busy every minute. Again, my thoughts flit to the retirement community and I realize that the healthy elders there, my parents for example, are similarly involved, sociable, keeping busy. These animals have much to teach me too. My job today is to watch and listen.

Our last sighting is a flock of flamingos, *Phoenicopterus*. My friend and I stare at the birds for a moment. At first glance I think they're not real, but those plastic statues people put in their yards. Bobbing necks and fluttering wings quickly make me revise my opinion.

"Which would you rather be?" my friend asks. "That big beautiful polar bear swimming so gracefully, or one of these silly, froufrou birds standing around on one leg?"

"The polar bear was beautiful," I admit. "But these guys are wearing pretty amazing ball gowns. Hot pink."

She shakes her head at me and we head off as the wind picks up and clouds gather overhead. It was a perfect afternoon at the zoo— many animals, much sunshine, beautiful fall leaves.

I hope the animals are as content, but I wonder. Electric fencing would not be required if the bears didn't have an urge to escape. This zoo doesn't have actual bars and cages—rather glass walls and steep cliffs and enclosures to keep everyone in the proper place. They have redesigned the environments and habitats to be more animal-friendly, but captivity is still captivity. At some level, I might prefer one of those extraordinary safari trips, where the humans are encased in a barred vehicle and the animals run free, but that's not in my budget. And yet, here these animals are alive and well-fed. The zoo staff seems uniformly kind and gentle. The endangered ones can reproduce and thrive here, perhaps to help repopulate the wilds. The non-endangered ones have been spared a cruel death by hunger or predation.

I wonder what the animals think of us, the visitors. We are strange, odd-smelling creatures who march about at the edges of their territories pushing wheeled machines or carrying cubs. Do they marvel at my bright blue sweater? Do they want to pat my friend's shiny pale hair?

. . . when a bear dies, something sacred in every living thing
interconnected with that realm . . . also dies.

—John Murray

in sickness and in health

MILKING A BEAR—just the phrase sets off an explosion of images and questions. How would you do it? Why would you do it? Doesn't all that fur get in the way? And how dangerous is it? I've never milked anything and don't intend to start unless my circumstances change dramatically.

When I was in college, a close friend spent a lot of her time milking pigs. She was a biology major studying immunology, specifically trying to discover what disease protection a mother pig hands down to her piglets via her milk. The friend has gone on to become a world-renowned virologist and immunologist, but we didn't know that back then.

My other friends and I got stuck on the actuality of milking pigs. First off, pig manure is really, really smelly. With cows or horses a barn has an earthy fragrance, and if the barn is well kept, it isn't unpleasant. With pigs, you want to be a mile or two down the road.

Then there's the physiology of pigs, the layout. Whereas a cow has an udder with four producing teats concentrated in a smallish area of the belly, the pig is really spread out. A sow has ten or twelve nipples arranged in two long rows. Convenient for nursing piglets—

as she may have a dozen offspring at one time, and they all have room to feed. But less convenient for the milking process. So of course we mocked our friend and teased her unmercifully. Imagined the construction of pig bras.

Cows are clearly a more common milk source than pigs, and this works well for both the dairy farmer and for the cow. A cow can produce large quantities of milk, more than her one or two offspring will consume. Left alone, her body will adjust itself to the demand of her calves but if a cow is part of a dairy operation, and if the farmer milks her morning and evening, she will produce anywhere from six to eight gallons each day. If she is not milked that frequently, she will complain by mooing loudly as the udder swells with excess milk. If this condition persists, she may even develop mastitis, an inflammation of the udder. So for a cow, the milking process leads to comfort and a reduction of pressure in the udder. It also keeps her mammary glands healthy.

☆

Our next neighbor to the north is a large dairy farm. My daughter and granddaughter and I make our way up the highway for an afternoon visit to the calf barn. These Jersey cows produce rich, creamy milk. They also produce very sweet calves.

We enter the calf barn's softly lit, fragrant aisles where small to medium-sized calves munch hay in their stalls. Our arrival causes a stir—shuffling and soft mooing. As I reach out to scratch the ears of a small brown baby, only two weeks old, she licks my hand with her long, narrow, snakey tongue. It tickles. My daughter and I both enjoy petting the animals, who want to taste and sniff us in return.

The granddaughter is another story. "Kiss, kiss," she says as the calves slurp our adult fingers. She likes it when dogs lick her fingers, but with the calves, she steps back out of reach and hides her hands behind her back. No surprise. Even the smallest are as tall as she is. Her afternoon perks up when she spies a barn cat sunning herself in a straw-filled wheelbarrow at the end of the aisle, a more manageable friend to pet.

If we stayed longer, we could watch the milking, but a couple of louder moos startle the little girl, so we make our way along the second aisle, making sure to scratch each pair of ears as we scuff past through the straw. Later we'll have milk from the mothers of these babies, and as a special treat, the rich, sweet, locally produced ice cream. All from my friendly neighborhood dairy farm.

☆

Once I encounter the notion of farming or milking a bear, I quickly wish I hadn't. For with bears, farming isn't about producing dairy products—it's about medicine, specifically, traditional Chinese medicine. My first introduction to these practices came via Lisa See, author of the Red Princess mystery series and other historical novels. But that was a fictional treatment. The facts have much more impact.

Traditional Chinese medicine places a high value on bear bile and bear gall as treatments for a variety of ills including fever, inflammation, digestive problems, eye irritation, gall stones, liver and heart disease. It is a popular ingredient in medicines in China, Japan, Korea, as well as in the United States and Canada in regions where large Asian communities flourish.

A bear gallbladder, obtained from a dead bear, can sell for $10,000 US in Korea for example. The organ is dried and ground into a fine powder before being mixed into various compounds. The Asiatic black bear, an endangered species, is a favored source, but various others, including the American black bear, are also harvested legally or illegally for the gall bladder. At the same time the hunter will often remove the bear's paws, an expensive culinary delicacy in many parts of Asia.

Bear *milking* is done not to obtain milk, but to obtain bile. Somewhere between eight and ten thousand live bears are currently being *farmed* in Asia for the production of bile. These bears are obtained as cubs, then caged in enclosures so small that an adult bear cannot fully stand or extend its body. The caged bears have injuries to their heads and faces, and broken teeth from trying to bite through the bars to escape.

The bear has a catheter attached to its gall bladder from which bile is syringed twice daily. This farming begins when the bear is three years of age and continues for the rest of its life. The life may not be as long as it would in the wild, however. Because of the cruel and unsanitary conditions on some farms, illness and infection is common.

☆

I am an omnivore—I enjoy eating meats and seafood along with my fruits and grains and vegetables. I love cheese. I am not opposed to the domestication and farming of animals, and to pretend those sensibilities while noshing on chicken barbeque would be dishonest. But I find the mistreatment of animals unconscionable, whether it occurs in Asian bear farms or American factory farms.

I cringe at stories of poultry bred for overlarge white meat—chickens who can't stand up because the breast portion is so heavy and out of scale with the rest of the body that it tips them over. Or the endless feedlots where cattle are fed corn, not their preferred grass or hay. These ruminants (cud chewers) don't digest the corn as readily as grasses, and so must be treated with various medicines, hormones, and chemicals to help them gain weight and come to full market size. As a matter of both conscience and taste, I try to avoid such sources of food for myself and my family.

Fortunately for me, there are alternatives—free range poultry, grass-fed beef. We humans are omnivores after all—our bodies are able to process both plant and animal products. So my compromise is to try to find foods that have been raised in a natural and kindly manner—animals that have had good lives followed by quick, clean, merciful deaths. Or, as a local farmer explains, "My turkeys have only one bad day."

We have visited his farm and it's true. He raises a wide variety of animals and they live in a green, lush environment with plenty of room to eat, play, grow. He even plows using oxen, rather than using gasoline- or diesel-fueled machines. His farm and the foods he produces are healthy and exceptionally tasty. I doubt I could eat my favorite delicious cheeses, for example, if the cow, goat or sheep producing the milk experienced the sort of ongoing pain that occurs in bear farms.

I cannot judge the choices made by others in different cultures. What choice would I make if I, or someone I loved, needed a particular medication to survive? If a bear-derived medicine might have saved my father-in-law from the slow erasure of Alzheimers, I doubt I would have scorned it. Likewise if it might have helped my mother-in-law avoid two hip replacements, if it might have prevented the deterioration of my father's mobility, or cured my mother's heart disease. Faced with such choices, my high moral principles would probably fly right out the window.

Ironically, the fact that I am alive to have those annoying, high moral principles is due in part to animal-based medicine. When my parents were first married they tried to start a family without success. The preferred strategy in those days was to prescribe an estrogen treatment for some number of months to help regularize a woman's ovulation cycle. This worked well for my mother, which is how she became my mother.

The estrogen was derived from the urine of pregnant mares. While urine is a waste product and naturally excreted, unlike bear bile, which must be removed in an invasive procedure, I'm guessing the mare was not all that comfortable when continuously hooked up to a urine collection bag. She would have been bred annually, and once pregnant, her movements would have been restricted to her stall. A harsh treatment for an animal who loves to run. Likewise, her water intake would have been limited, so that she would produce more concentrated urine.

When I think about how much I hated the hormonal ups and downs of two pregnancies, how anxious I was to resume normal life, it occurs to me that I should feel sorry for those long ago, thirsty horses. Sorry and grateful.

Over time, drug producers have instituted stricter standards to produce a quality drug, and to protect the horses. Still, some animal activists oppose the production of equine-based estrogens on the grounds of cruelty. On the other side of that argument are birth control pills, hormone replacement therapy, and fertility treatments, resulting in an unknown number of people who wouldn't be here without those horses. Like me.

As with horse-derived estrogen, scientists are trying to develop kinder methods of producing bear-type medicines and are studying alternatives. Various herbal and plant-based treatments are beginning to replace bear bile and gall products. Fewer people in these markets approve of using bear products than in the past (only 30 percent approve these days; 70 percent disapprove), and more are willing to use other medicines. Finally, ursodeoxycholic acid (the active ingredient in bear bile) can now be synthesized. Perhaps the next generations will use alternative medicines. And perhaps this is good news for the people and for the bears.

Bears keep me humble. They help me to keep the world in perspective and to understand where I fit on the spectrum of life.

—Wayne Lynch

bears in the library

I WAS AN über tree-girl in my cub years. To this day, my daughters scold me for animal abuse because, when I was about eight or nine, I'd carry my small dog in one arm up into the branches of an old apple tree in the side yard. It wasn't abusive in the least, as a.) the tree wasn't very tall and therefore not scary; b.) the dog wasn't very heavy, so not in danger of being dropped; and c.) she was my dog and she liked to spend time with me, so of course she loved the tree as much as I did.

We'd sit there for a while, me on the branch, dog on my lap, and soak up the fresh air. She understood and commiserated with me when I'd been scolded by my parents and needed a little time outdoors with trees to help me feel better. In my universe, the right dog and the right tree can make just about anybody feel better. The trick is not to tell your daughters about it.

As I grew older and stronger, I became a tree racer. At the corner of our property stood an old locust tree bent by the wind so that it leaned out over the yard; one thick branch grew horizontally, parallel to the ground. I'd get a running start, scamper up the leaning trunk, grab hold and swing around to the horizontal branch, then scramble out to the very end, drop down, grip the branch and jump. My father timed me—I could do the entire trip in less than a minute.

☆

In our library, a framed print of bears presides above a shelf of non-fiction, a pair of large-eared cubs perched in a tree. I love this picture, partly because the cubs are very sweet, and partly because of my own history with trees.

The print is a hand-me-down from my mother-in-law, so the matting and framing look a little tired, but the image itself is charming. We have a folk art motif going in the room—all paneled in wormy chestnut, it needs the lightness and whimsy of primitive artwork. So the bears fit in fine, or they will once I replace the mat and frame. And replace them I will. I want to keep those cubs in sight, especially if there's a good chance we'll lose the real ones, either to a rifle shot, or to the natural progression of maturity and moving on. Mother bears do take the empty nest seriously and banish their maturing cubs to find their own territories.

Many bears live in my library. I relish John Irving's writing. The fiction lover in me appreciates his humor, originality, his wildly imagined plots. The writer in me applauds the way he can be compassionate, kind, and generous to his characters, quirks, flaws and all. I admire the way his people show defiance in the face of doom and darkness. And then there are the bears, which appear and cause havoc in many, many of his novels.

Authors as widely diverse as Robert McCloskey (*Blueberries for Sal*), Jean Auel (*The Clan of the Cave Bear*), Bill Bryson (*A Walk in the Woods*), poet Mary Oliver (*Spring*), and William Faulkner (*The Bear*) give bears starring roles, as does a new story cycle by Alice Hoffman, *The Red Garden*, in which an iconic bear is the centrifugal force around which all the stories spin.

My husband informs me that there are bears in the world of classical music as well. In Richard Wagner's *Siegfried*, the title character makes friends with a wild bear in act one. Perhaps this is not quite as dramatic as the triumphal parade with an elephant in act two of Verdi's *Aida*, but it's dramatic enough for me.

Bela Bartok included "The Bear Dance" as the second movement in a solo piano work, *Sonatina on Romanian Folk Tunes*. This folk dance, also called the "Russian Bear Dance" has many incarnations; some pantomime the hunting of a bear while others include a human dressed as a bear in the festivities. In most versions, good looking and athletic young men squat down near the floor and kick their legs out quickly then return to the squatting position. It takes excellent balance, coordination and endurance. It also burns the quads.

Then there are the bears who show up in the sports pages. Here in Massachusetts, the Boston Bruins are favorite sons, even though most of these hockey players come from Canada. Teams with bear mascots range from the professional Chicago Bears to the fictional Bad News Bears. Chicago must be as bear-crazy as I am for they have both Bears who play football and Cubs who swat baseballs in Wrigley Field, a ballpark named for chewing gum. Which leads me to speculate about bears and chewing gum. Yup, they'd probably swallow it.

I'm guessing these sports names were derived from the size and perceived power of real bears. But the mascot-namers got much of it wrong. Bears are not team players—they're solitary—and when large males are surrounded by other large males they will most likely fight amongst themselves, not create an impenetrable offensive line to protect their quarterback or work together to complete the perfect double play. And in spite of their size and strength, black bears are generally not ferocious. They'd just as soon disappear into the woods or find a ripe berry patch as engage in conflict. They might stomp and snort a bit, but they'd rather eat than fight.

☆

I'm in the library contemplating a gold-finish frame and creamy mat because summer is over. The sun porch is now cold; the chill of its bluestone floor, so welcome during August, now makes the arch of my foot ache. The library is our cold-weather gathering place.

I'm still pondering bears. Since I haven't personally sighted one this summer, I'm hoping that perhaps it may happen in the fall. It's been warm—the trees are only now showing full color in the third week of October and the roses are still blooming—so surely nobody is hibernating yet.

Do I really want to see a bear or three? My daughter is visiting along with her daughter. Do I want a bear to frighten this small, joyful girl? Absolutely not. So perhaps at naptime?

I head outside to collect logs for the fireplace. We had a big, old, shagbark hickory, *Carya ovata,* split vertically from top to bottom this summer, probably a delayed result of the huge windstorm. It eventually dropped in two halves and has been cut to fireplace lengths. While most of the logs will require a full year to dry and season, the splintered edges near the top of the trunk along the split are already quite brittle. They make great kindling.

I am out filling the bucket with hickory shreds, surrounded by flaming leaves in russet and gold, when I hear the familiar crashing of branches that announces the passage of a large, heavy animal in the woods to the south.

It sounds pretty close. I scan the woods and, sure enough, see motion among limbs and branches. More crashing. I'm close enough to the house that I don't feel personally threatened, so wonder what to do. Should I rush inside and tell everyone to at least look out the windows? I'm tempted, for surely my husband and daughter want to see the bears—none of us has seen a full family grouping thus far. But if I leave my woodpile, the bears may disappear and I won't see them myself.

I choose the selfish option and stay planted, watching intently. And then it appears—a largish, six foot shape, but not a furry black bear. A man. My husband, in fact, wearing a flannel shirt and wielding a shovel.

I put the puzzle together slowly. He has come out during naptime to remove the fresh carcass of a raccoon who showed up as road kill on the edge of the driveway this morning, so it doesn't upset our youngest visitor. I don't need to announce the presence of a crashing hulk to him—he is the crashing hulk. All of which seems ludicrous and completely in tune with this week in the country. We are giggling and singing our way through each day.

The giggling grows louder and more intense when my husband checks the weather on the computer and sees the teaser about a bear cub in a grocery store. Sure enough, a video shows a small cub who has wandered into an IGA store in Ketchikan, Alaska, and is dancing back and forth atop the produce racks. Finally, a guy grabs it by the nape and carries it back outside to the woods. The cub's cries sound like a small child's. I can't help wondering what happens to all those trod-upon vegetables.

So I don't see any live bears, just a filmed one. But I do hope the bears find the raccoon. It might make a good snack. Bad outcome for the raccoon, but good news for the bears.

☆

We've had another summer of no bear sighting. But no rifle shots either. Old trees have come down, but we're planting new ones. Our family includes a generation in each of life's four seasons. Spring: the youngest in our family are growing and thriving, perhaps like those unseen cubs. Summer: the children's parents are doing what parents everywhere do—taking care of their young and preparing them to live independent, rich, adult lives someday. Winter: three of our parents are surviving, surmounting obstacles and clinging to life with a certain bearlike tenacity.

And the rest of us, autumnals, well, we're hanging in. Hiking the woods. Smelling woodsmoke. Making soups. Watching for bears. Living in the world, and loving it.

☆

Somewhere a black bear has just risen from sleep and is
staring down the mountain . . .

—Mary Oliver

☆

what needs to be done: redux

SOMETIMES IT'S HARD to tell the truth, especially for a professional liar. And a fiction writer is, after all, just such a liar. I make up stories, invent entire populations of characters to inhabit those stories, and create tons of conflict to throw at these made-up people. If I do a good enough job—if my lies are convincing and believable—publishers actually pay me money, in the form of royalties, for such misbehavior. It's great fun. I know this because most of my books are fiction. Nonfiction, on the other hand, requires fidelity—a faithfulness to the truth, even when a small invention would make the story so much more fun.

☆

On a Saturday afternoon in mid-June we have weekend guests. Most are out with my husband; only one is home with me, and she's napping due to a nasty cold. We have all spoken about the bear, but the bear hasn't chosen to share her presence. I have a sense that some of our visitors may see my bear tales as apocryphal.

Then my neighbor, Dina, calls. "The bear's here again, coming your way, right toward your porch. Stay inside."

"I will." I hurry to hang up the phone and rush to the sun porch. Sure enough that familiar shape is ambling in my direction. I toy with the idea of waking my guest—surely she'd love to see this bear. But she's also been feeling stuffy and terrible and could use the sleep. So I don't bother her.

Instead, I watch the bear. She's alone, which means her cubs of last summer have grown and are now independent and living in their own territories. Because it's June, this also means she's probably in estrus, prowling, looking for mates. She's beautiful, so she should have no trouble in that endeavor. Her fur shines in the afternoon sun as she makes her slow, steady progress toward my windows. I watch as her face comes into clear view—long snout pointing right toward me. As she passes by the boxwoods, at most ten feet from where I stand, I follow, slipping from window to window. Now I see her in profile, large, and polished as coal.

Stay inside, my neighbor has warned and I do, although I have a perverse temptation to go out and greet this creature whom I have come to see as a friend. The sensible part of my brain cautions that while I may see her as a friend, this bear probably has a completely different opinion of me.

Minutes pass—three—five. She's moving slowly, almost promenading as if she senses an audience. At last she angles away from the house and toward the front yard trees. I step through the kitchen and then into the dining room in pseudo pursuit. I stand guard by the corner window, watching, until the last shadow of her shape disappears into the larger shadows of the spruces and pines.

Seconds later my human guest appears in the hallway.

"You just missed the bear." I point toward the front yard.

"Oh, rats. I should have come down sooner. I've been awake for a while."

"I should have called you down, sorry."

As she fixes herself some herbal tea, I hop online and email a close friend who knows of my fascination with all things *ursidae. The bear came by just now. It's gonna be a great summer!*

Which just goes to show how wrong I can be—how badly I've misinterpreted this omen, both in the short and long term. A few minutes pass and I see my neighbor's husband outdoors and decide to pop out to chat. Bear sightings are worth sharing.

"She's back," he says.

"I know. I watched her."

"It must be me," he continues, shaking his head. "I was here exactly a year ago and she broke into the garage. Now I'm back from Afghanistan and she breaks in again."

"What? She broke in? I didn't . . ."

"Oh, yeah. I heard this noise—rattling the door—just like the last time. She only got her head and front paws into the garage this time. And no cubs. But I scared her off."

"Whoa." I don't know what else to say. They are packing up to move to his new posting, in a tropical locale where there will be no bears, and also no war zone.

I make a note to myself to have a sturdy pair of latches installed right away as we'll soon have new neighbors, older folks who don't need this sort of hassle, not that anyone does. Then I realize how foolish my email now sounds. A break-in is not just a sighting.

☆

Our guests leave late on Sunday morning, and my husband catches a ride with them. I'm on my own again and will be for a few days before a new crop of friends, students, and family arrive. Before that can happen, a call comes from Ohio. My mother's health is in question. Calls like this have been coming off and on for several months, and it's hard to tell when the situation is serious and when it's minor. I visited in late May, before coming to Massachusetts, and things seemed fine then.

I spend a morning pondering what to do as I yank weeds from the biggest of my gardens. Then I realize that this activity, which usually calms me, isn't working. I'm worried and anxious, so pack quickly, cancel the rest of my June plans, and head west that afternoon. Two days later I am in Ohio, for what will be one of many trips this summer. So again, the bear sighting hasn't brought good luck but the exact opposite.

Family concerns keep me occupied, so I can't be in town to greet our new neighbors when they arrive in early July. We converse via email and I have to make sure they're aware of the bear and that they'll keep their cat safely indoors. The bear is less of a threat to a feline than the coyotes who skulk about up on the mountain, but in either case, I don't want them to put their pet at risk. I do make sure they know how to contact our property manager, and I assure them that the lawn guy will be watching out for the property in general, and for the bear in particular.

Wrong again. Rick is one of my best friends in the country; he's the guy who is planning to *do what needs to be done* . . . He's part of my safety net, one of the many kind men who help us manage a second home property at a distance from our main residence. And then I return from a midsummer trip to Ohio only to hear his brother's voice on our answering machine. *Call me.*

When I do, the news is devastating: Rick has had a stroke, a big one. This lean, muscular guy who wrestles trees to the ground, this ex-Marine, is now flat-out himself, in a medically induced coma. When he regains any consciousness at all, he fights and rages, risking further damage. It will take days for his system to calm, weeks and months for him to begin to recover.

It's painful to deal with the illness of an elderly parent. In a different way I struggle with Rick's condition. He's a few years younger than I am, so the risk feels much more personal, more in my face, more this-could-happen-to-me. And I worry about our new tenants, about being a careless landlord.

I swallow hard and think about my bear sighting. Only a few weeks have passed, but it now seems so long ago—that naïveté, that hopefulness. One, two, three strikes and I'm out.

The bear has definitely won this round.

☆

In real life, when an odd set of circumstances occurs, if it is favorable to us, we're delighted with our good fortune. In fiction, such circumstantial happenings are judged by the phrase *deus ex machina,* loosely translated as *God is the machine, God made it happen.* These acts of God point to a writer who has painted herself into a corner and can't find a way out; they are unbelievable, unrealistic and usually must be excised from the manuscript. The opposite applies as well—trouble and conflict are unwelcome in real life, but are the very heart of fiction.

The shape of this summer has the feel of fiction—three events building tension and ongoing drama—like something I've constructed. Except that I haven't; the events are all coincidental, a break-in and two separate, distant illnesses. It's one thing to create happenings for an invented set of characters; it's totally different when tough things occur in real life to those I care about. So as story-shaped as the summer has been, it's all true. And in the telling, I am trying to behave like my friend Rick, the ex-Marine—*semper fi*—always faithful, to the truth. No lie.

☆

All is number . . .

—Pythagoras

☆

bears by the numbers

YOGI BEAR WOULD be so proud—seventy-eight Jellystone Park Camp Resorts (franchised) are located across the US and Canada, where families can camp, stay in RVs or cabins, and have an outdoorsy good time. Wisconsin leads the list with seven sites; my home state of Pennsylvania has four; my part-time state of Massachusetts has two. These camping areas cluster near tourist attractions with lots of open space or wilderness—New York's Catskill Mountains, as opposed to Times Square for example. Hard to imagine pitching a tent on all that concrete.

Likewise, real black bears spread themselves liberally across the continent concentrating in areas with open space and plenty of forest. Also hard to imagine bears denning up in Times Square on all that concrete with all those fashionable New Yorkers rushing about in high-heeled boots.

Just as Yogi's Jellystone Camping Resorts stretch from California to Maine and Florida, so black bears inhabit forty-one states and all Canadian Provinces except Prince Edward Island where they have been eliminated. No wild bears reportedly live in North Dakota, South Dakota, Nebraska, Kansas. Iowa, Illinois, Indiana, Delaware, and certainly none in Hawaii. A few live in Ohio (seventy), Alabama (fifty), Rhode Island (ten). Texas, which usually announces itself in a loud voice, whispers about bears. Estimates of Texas bears range from fifty to two hundred fifty known animals in recent years.

Alaska leads the continent at two hundred thousand bears followed by British Columbia (120–160,000), Ontario (65–75,000) and Wisconsin (26–40,000). All these high populations occur in places with significant forested land—good bear habitat. The non-bear states include prairie lands where grasses and farms predominate and trees are ornamental.

☆

All across North America bear biologists are singing a new song and I must learn this difficult music. Fresh lyrics include: harvest; conflict avoidance; population control; awareness; management. Before and during much of the twentieth century, many species of animals declined in population, some to dangerous levels. Because of expanding human populations, unregulated hunting, expanding agriculture, logging and the building of highways and railroads, many of the forest dwellers' and edge species' numbers shrank dramatically.

Beginning in the 1970s, through conservation laws and policy, wildlife biologists actively sought to protect these animal species. In many cases, white-tailed deer or coyotes, for example, they succeeded beyond imagining. Deer have become pests, the rats of the forest. Coyotes slink about at the edges of heavily populated cities and suburbs from ocean to ocean.

At the same time, forests themselves have been re-growing, especially in the northeast, where rocky, hardscrabble farms have returned to the wild. Many favorite Berkshire Mountain wilderness hikes pass by old stone foundations and skirt still-visible, still-standing, stone walls. These woodlands increase animal habitat opportunities. Research from 2007 suggests that 747,000 black bears live in the US and Canada.

Now wildlife and game commissions must work in a different dimension and must at some level undo their earlier efforts. While they continue to encourage human populations to admire and respect wildlife, they also push for a realistic sort of coexistence. If human admiration includes anthropomorphism and sentimentality—the Bambi effect, *poor little deer, a mean old hunter killed his mommy*—it can stand in the way of achieving a healthy balance between human and animal communities. The consequences of doing nothing may include overgrazing, encroachment on human communities by wild animals, adaptation to human food sources, conflict.

A new vocabulary is emerging. Harvest equals hunting, a primary and cost-effective solution to overpopulation. Some states allow large animal hunting both fall and spring. Biologists set hunting license numbers, based on population statistics—they increase license availability when the animal numbers increase to overload. The license fees help support the work of managing and maintaining wild places.

Hunting is challenging in populated areas, however. Most people don't want hunters discharging firearms in their backyards, even though suburban and exurban developments are very attractive to wildlife—the edge between forest and clearings are a preferred terrain for deer, wild turkeys, coyotes. Some communities permit bow and arrow hunting, or the use of sharpshooters—often police—to reduce herd or flock sizes, but many do not. Meanwhile, people grow angry and take up polarized positions—*we must control these nuisances* or *we must protect nature in all shapes and sizes.*

Other forms of population control are less effective. In many regions, especially in the eastern half of the country, we have eliminated natural predation by wiping out alpha predators such as wolves and mountain lions. But even they may not be effective with animals as large as the black bear. Some predators (coyotes or wolves in packs) do take out cubs, but rarely full-grown bears. Disease isn't a major factor in bear mortality. They're a healthy lot, those bruins and they have few enemies except us.

Birth control, tried with deer, is expensive and hit or miss. Sterilization with return to the wild has been tried with feral cats, but while individual cats may not bear kittens, these felines show no sign of declining numbers. And there aren't a lot of celibate critters out there—instinct tells them to reproduce and further their species.

Bears are successful reproducers. A female may live for twenty years in the wild. She will begin reproducing at approximately three or four years of age. Average litter size is three cubs every two years. The survival rate for cubs in the wild is about 60-75 percent; those who don't survive often die due to small size or inadequate food supplies. Doing the math for just one female's primary offspring, she will reproduce eight times for a total of twenty-four live births, fifteen of which will survive to maturity. If half of those cubs are female, she's going to have several generations of matrilineal, female, reproducing offspring during her lifetime—eight daughters and more than fifty in the generations that follow during her twenty-year lifespan. A prolific babe indeed.

If we humans reproduced at such a rate it would sink the planet in two or three generations—imagine a woman who could reproduce from ages 13 to 50, generating a baby a year until the equipment gives out. Fortunately we bear mostly single births and our long childhoods reduce the multiplier effect seen in the bears, but it's still sobering. In my own growing up years, I knew a number of families with seven, ten, thirteen children—not at all unusual. Things have changed—humans do use birth control successfully, so successfully in fact that folks in the United States are having a hard time just generating replacements for themselves. Makes me wonder how long it might take for the bears to overtake us.

Hunting practices and regulations for bears in most states run counter to all this numerical logic. For the trophy hunter, the large male is the preferred target, but as in most animal populations having fewer males doesn't seriously impact population growth. Even for the food hunter, who may prefer a younger, more tender meat source, the shooting or harvesting of females with cubs or of cubs is outlawed. Yet the reduction of actual or potential breeders would improve overpopulation numbers. And it would reduce the number of nuisance animals—many of which are dispersing adolescents in search of their own home territories. Bears aged one to five account for 70 percent of the bear-human conflict.

Conflict avoidance is a critical aspect of wildlife management. Or how do I keep from hitting a deer/moose with my car and killing either the animal or myself and surely damaging my vehicle? How do I keep the bears from breaking into the garage, yet again? Overgrazing deer are the bane of many communities, while some lakes and ponds have serious pollution conditions due to non-migratory wild geese population excesses and the resulting muck they deposit so generously. My nephew calls one nearby swimming area Goose Poop Beach.

Awareness—human awareness—and education is critical. Human food is a magnet for wild animals. Our richly available commodities provide them with more calories for less effort than wild food sources, whether it's birdseed in the feeder, dog food in the garage bin, or domestic cats—yum, coyotes love them. Good information can help people avoid some of the worst mistakes, such as intentionally feeding wild animals or not properly protecting human food and garbage and pets.

Management strategies at the state level currently look at numbers and statistics so we can make choices based on information rather than guesses. So we can care for the animals and the people that coexist in towns, cities, and rural regions.

☆

I'm all for that—for coexistence—between people and animals and between people and people. On an international and national level, I'd like to see more tolerance and less conflict. More debates and fewer wars. More exchange students and fewer exchanges of gunfire.

Folks in our family have a broad variety of political opinions and religious opinions—those hot topics that used to be forbidden at the dinner table as the arguments that might ensue would ruin one's digestion. We mostly don't club each other over the head but instead try to disagree with respect, even when every sort of media urges polarization and demonization of the opposing side. It seems the media have not heard of checks and balances. That they don't understand the notion that no one side is right all the time. That we all need to have our ideas and beliefs refreshed from time to time.

I can't envision myself as a hunter of wildlife except with a camera. Still I believe that most hunters share my commitment to conservation of wild places—that we speak some of the same language even if we enjoy different outdoor activities.

Perhaps we're following the example of Teddy Roosevelt, a soldier, adventurer, naturalist, big game hunter and our first conservationist president. Roosevelt established the National Forest Service, several national parks and preserves, as well as historically significant monuments. As president, he set aside more land for preservation than all previous presidents combined. Due to his foresight, his love for the outdoors, all Americans, hunters and non-hunters alike, have access to wild places, to forested lands. I'm grateful. Without the forests, we would live more depleted lives.

As a meat-eater, I also don't engage in arguments with vegetarians or vegans. I believe in choices and that a number of people, when given the same information, might come to different conclusions. I believe we are all enriched by the diversity we encounter in the world, whether diversity of opinion and thought among our human brothers and sisters, or diversity among the flora and fauna that surround us.

For me, the world is a smorgasbord, a rich array. Like the bears in my woods and my yard, I'd rather taste and nibble and savor than waste time in unnecessary battles. I can be firm and ferocious when that's called for, but in most of my life, it is seldom called for. In the meantime it's a big world out there—and as master chef Julia Child often said, *bon appetite!*

☆

A-you're adorable, B-you're so beautiful, C-you're a cutie full of charms . . .

—Buddy Kaye and Fred Wise

☆

the cuteness conundrum

I'M A PROFESSIONAL writer. I try to avoid repeating myself unless it happens intentionally, for emphasis, in a poem or a short picture book text. Yet as I sit and compose these essays, I keep bumping into the word "cute." My editor likewise has highlighted it in an early draft, but not critically at all. She wants more.

I'm not sure about that. For me, always stuck in the front row for class pictures as a child, now a petite woman who can't reach the high shelves in the kitchen, I bristle at cute. It feels demeaning, diminutive, a verbal cue for taking someone—usually a female—less seriously. Rumor has it that adult men who retain a youthful face may also be treated as if still children. Given a choice of descriptors, I might choose elegant or glamorous, but nobody's really offering those choices.

I'm always pleased when, after participating in a meeting or discussion, I stand up and someone says, "Oh, you're short. I thought you were taller."

"I have a tall voice," I explain. So yes, I probably overcompensate. Not as badly as Napoleon Bonaparte, but still.

Most of what we find cute includes, in addition to small size, some aspect of physical attractiveness, whether in the home or out in the wider world. Beauty seems to have survival value in nature. Beautiful flowering plants attract pollinators. Many animals perform exhibitionist mating rituals, flaunting fur or plumage or body parts, or in the case of people, all of the above—that bikini-clad woman with long shiny hair strutting her stuff poolside. And the cute cuddly offspring that result are hard to resist. We want to hug them and love them, whether child or cub or cria. Which helps to keep this old world and us, its inhabitants, alive.

☆

My dictionary helps me out with *cute*. It offers three meanings: prettily dainty, as in cute bunny or cute hat which is fine for hats and bunnies, but not so great for adults; annoyingly mincing as when one tries too hard and overdoes it which I equate with cutesie and try to avoid even more assiduously; and clever or shrewd, which I like when used as a one word snark in a low-pitched voice accompanied by a raised eyebrow and a scowl—cute.

I suspect there's more meaning here than the dictionary supplies. *Bartlett's Quotations* has no entry for cute, not a single one. Evidently the giants of the literary canon did not use the word. But where Bartlett's comes up empty, Google overflows. The search engine overwhelms me and therefore offers no help at all. I plug in *cute* and I'm instantly referred to hundreds of sappy, insipid phrases about friendship, romantic love, adorable words to include in a tattoo, and so on. And then the photographs—over the top. Only one site, Attack of the Cute shares any of my irritation with the phenomenon by allowing viewers to rate images of small creatures, human and otherwise, using the following scale: *It's so cute; It's so fluffy; meh.* Door number one, *It's so cute,* wins most of the votes, but somehow I lean toward the *meh* folks. The photos are extraordinarily contrived.

And yet . . . and yet, I'm drawn to authentic cuteness, as in my grandchildren and small critters of many sorts. And I think that's the key—when one is young and small and cute, it's fine. But as time passes, yeah, *grow up!*

There may be an evolutionary advantage to infant cuteness—it may engender a protective and loving response in parents. But why is that? How does it work? Reiner Sprengelmeyer of the University of St. Andrews and colleagues elsewhere studied reactions of female and male humans to human babies to try to discover the science behind that vague notion. They found that females of childbearing age and those taking the hormone estrogen responded more strongly than did males or post-menopausal women to overt signs of infant cuteness —large heads, large eyes, chubby cheeks. In my mind this connects to the fact that male black bears are known to attack and kill cubs, but females are not. Similarly, male lions and male mice and some kinds of fish can destroy the young of their species.

I sense that the protective value of cuteness goes beyond the infancy stage. Human toddlers too are cute, and thank goodness for it because they can also be exasperating and exhausting—active every minute, demanding, prone to temper tantrums and fixated on the word NO! But we love them anyway if they're related to us or if they're behaving themselves in public. We love them less when they cry on airplanes or in restaurants—if they're ours we get grumpy, but if they belong to strangers we get irate.

For me, the cuteness quotient extends into a good number of other creatures. Small furry mammals have great appeal. There's no comparison, for example, between a two-week-old little spotted piglet and its mother. The sow is just that, a huge female hog that smells bad and grunts. But the piglet is charming. Likewise, while many people eat beef, a number of beef-eaters balk at eating veal— young calves. Sometimes it's an intellectual choice, based on the way some calves are raised—in the dark, in constrained environments where they can't exercise and toughen their muscles. But I'm guessing the cuteness factor also plays a part in the choice—the Bambi effect again.

Big creatures, like my bears, go from being cute cubs to beautiful or majestic or awesome or intimidating. Animals that stay small even when mature, like rabbits, hold on to their winsome appeal. When was the last time you saw an intimidating rabbit?

Among the birds, newborns don't appeal to me much. Once they fluff out, fine, but the chick stage doesn't last long. Overall birds can be beautiful, powerful, graceful, streamlined. Rarely are they cute. Even tiny hummingbirds with their bright feathers have aggressive personalities and thereby escape the cute label.

Cold-blooded reptiles don't score very high on my cute-o-meter either. I hate snakes. Yes, I know they eat lots of small rodents and I appreciate it—they lower the population of field mice seeking winter homes in my house. But I'd prefer that the snakes do their hunting and their sunning upon rocks out of my line of vision.

I do like amphibians, even though they're also cold-blooded. That tree frog, *Hyla arborea,* with its suction-cup feet that grapples onto my screen door during a summer rainstorm, for example. But the amphibian appeal is less about beauty and more about oddness—a quirkiness or humor or character, the way a frog or toad blinks and looks serious, the way a salamander darts about, the way a cluster of small turtles goes plop-plop-plop from log into river as I paddle past in my kayak.

I don't think of most insects as cute, although some seem beautiful—especially the flittery ones like the blue dragonflies that light on my knee, or butterflies, or the more colorful beetles with vibrant markings. And I like bees—not wasps or hornets, but honeybees and especially bumblebees as they stagger like drunks from flower to flower. Mosquitoes, cockroaches, millipedes, stinkbugs? You can have them. All.

☆

Small and miniature seems to fascinate people, and not just children—doll houses, train sets, matchbox cars—as we age these items go from toys to collectibles to valuables. We even have a category of cute foods. While miniaturization of food is relatively recent in the US, Japanese mothers have been creating tiny works of art for their children's lunch boxes for some time. Kawaii cooking, Bento or Obento, is the art of making creatures from rice and decorating them with tiny bits of meat, cheese, vegetables or seaweed, then sculpting fruits and vegetables into flowers and fanciful designs to make a chef-worthy presentation, all in a reusable Bento box. To an adult they seem too beautiful to eat, and they obviously take lot of time to prepare. But to children, perhaps they invite the tongue to try new tastes and eat healthy, fresh foods. The Bento tradition is being translated for American cooks and their hungry children, again with an emphasis on healthy, fresh ingredients.

The small-is-good food trend is catching on elsewhere in our society. Except at a Chinese restaurant, it used to be awkward to exchange tastes across the white tablecloth when eating out. The bread plate served as conveyance. Now, tapas and small plate menus similarly invite the diner to explore several different tastes in a single meal, without having to worry about dropping a sticky chunk of chicken enroute across the table. You can order sliders (pint-sized burgers) in various meat and flavor choices, purchase mini carrots (healthy) or bite-sized candy bars (not so healthy).

The world of appetizers has similarly exploded. Years ago mini-quiches showed up, an exciting innovation. Now you can find recipes for lasagna cupcakes, mac and cheese cupcakes, baby chicken pot-pies, teeny grilled cheese sandwiches, meatloaf cupcakes frosted with a dab of mashed potato, all of which make that slider look large. The list goes on, with all of these tiny concoctions prepared in mini-muffin pans, the same mini-muffin pans one uses to bake those miniature cupcakes, which are so delightful. Ironic, though, that while cute, Lilliputian foods seem to be a rising fad, nationally obesity and childhood obesity are epidemic.

When lunching with friends and splurging on something naughty and sweet, I often declare that no calories are involved if splitting a dessert. All the calories go to the other person. Perhaps a similar deceptive force is at work with mini-foods. They're so small and so cute, I could eat a dozen. And so I do. Oops.

As Gulliver found himself constantly hungry in the land of Lilliput, so too would bears probably find intentionally tiny foods illogical and downright frustrating. They must consume what nature provides, often nuts and berries which come in small doses. And so like me, they eat dozens and dozens. But bears work it off. I might not, but I probably won't grow taller either, just a bit pudgier. And wouldn't that be cute!

No. It would not.

*Swallow a toad in the morning if you want to encounter
nothing more disgusting the rest of the day . . .*

—Nicolas Chamfort

close encounters of the furred kind

WHILE I SPEND a summer in travel—Massachusetts, Pennsylvania,
Ohio, and delightfully, Scotland—bears too are on the move, this
time in Pittsburgh. They aren't so much visiting family or playing
tourist, they're heading for the mall. It's a true story that feels like a
movie script.

During July 2012, a young 125-pound female enters a Sears store
via one of those automatic doors. Well designed for people pushing
strollers or walkers, or for teenagers with bags filled with back-to-
school wardrobes, these doors open gracefully when a pedestrian
approaches. Even if the pedestrian is a good-sized bear, albeit one
with a faulty fashion sense. If she were a hipster of a bear, she wouldn't
choose Sears.

The young bear has been seen days earlier in the nearby woods,
and heads toward a Walmart and then a J.C. Penney store during the
afternoon. She later finds herself in the parking lot where cars chase
and probably frighten her. Eventually she enters the Sears Grand
store in the evening—an all-night sale perhaps? Help comes in the
form of mall security who close the mall, and then wildlife conservation officers who are able to trap the bear between two sets of
glass doors.

They take aim with a tranquillizer weapon and fire twice at the bear, but she stays in motion. She reenters the store and staggers around perusing the electronics, clearly affected by the medication, but not yet immobile. Perhaps she's interested in a new video game. Or else watching *Animal Planet* on one of those gigantic televisions. In either case, bears metabolize the tranquillizer drugs quickly so effectiveness varies based on the animal's weight and activity level; it can take multiple doses to knock a bear out.

People (sales clerks and employees, I'm presuming, as the mall has been closed to the public) gather and take videos and pictures with their phones. This continues for forty-five minutes until the young bear finally drops to the floor, and the wildlife officers can haul her out to a waiting bear trap trailer. She is wearing a tracking collar, so may be part of a research study. End of story.

Not quite. A couple of hours later, a large, mature female enters the Sears store through the exact same set of automatic doors. This time they close the mall and attempt to corral the bear but are unsuccessful. She wanders around for a spell, then escapes. She too is wearing a tracking collar and causes a traffic jam when she meanders along a nearby highway.

While the wildlife conservation officers aren't willing to draw conclusions about relationships between the two bears, I'm guessing the second bear is the first bear's mother, following a clear and familiar scent trail. And as sometimes happens with a human mother and a teenaged daughter, shopping sprees must be curtailed. *No new fancy phone this week, sorry.* I just hope mother and daughter are both safe and perhaps reunited, although the juvenile is probably being fledged this summer in any case and should be seeking her own territory.

☆

Meanwhile, in Glendale, California, near where my daughter lives and works, another bear is busy. The so-called Glendale Bear has been spotted repeatedly in this lovely neighborhood north of downtown

Los Angeles near the mountains. The bear has been subdued and transported twice, but keeps coming back. On most of his trips, people scatter to get out of the way, but once they reach a safe distance, they pull out their phones to take pictures and videos.

One young man, however, doesn't have a clue. He's busy using his phone to text or talk to someone and is caught on video walking head-on, almost straight into the face of the Glendale Bear. He looks up, completely startled, then does the worst thing possible—he turns and runs. Fortunately the bear doesn't give chase so the young man isn't physically harmed, but surely some degree of psychological injury is inflicted when one's dumb behavior goes viral on the internet.

As the summer progresses, the Glendale Bear is caught once again, and relocated to an animal preserve. Its days in the wild are over. No more photo ops for the neighbors. No more close encounters of the furred kind.

☆

Not everyone ignores the bear nearby. In New Mexico this same summer a black truck backs toward a small dumpster by the side of a country road. In the truck bed, a woman wearing a pink shirt wrestles with a ladder as the truck nears the dumpster. A large black bear has been guarding the dumpster and she puts some distance between herself and the truck, but still prowls nearby.

Once the truck stops, the woman hoists the ladder into the dumpster, jiggles it a bit and lets go. The truck pulls away. Immediately little heads pop up—three black bear cubs. The mother bear returns to the dumpster as the first baby climbs out and hops to the ground. The other two climb more cautiously up and out and join the parade as Mama leads her troops down the road and out of sight.

From the descriptions that accompany this video, the cubs were crying while trapped in the dumpster and the man and woman with the truck figured out how to help reunite this bear family, so went home for the ladder. They expected a single cub rescue but instead got three. The moral of these stories: if you're going to have thousands of internet hits, make sure you're doing a good deed on camera, not making a fool of yourself.

☆

Across the country, black bears are increasing in population and humans are encroaching on the wilderness. Put those two facts together and it becomes clear that more and more encounters will occur, either when bears enter what seems to be our turf, or when we're traveling through theirs.

Most of the time the encounters will be brief and not particularly dangerous. They will be exciting and memorable and may produce a great story for the family.

Most of the time the bear will be following the scent of food, either his or ours. If we've done our job and handled our food and trash sensibly, the bear will sniff and walk away.

Most of the time, even if a bear appears to come after a person, it is a challenging behavior, a bluff charge, not a dangerous one. The bear may be simply saying, *Back off. You're getting too close. I need some space here.*

The wise person listens. She looks large and backs away. She lives to tell the tale. The unwise person does none of the above.

He is to me like a bear lying in wait, like a lion in hiding . . .

—Lamentations 3:10

unholy bears

THREE HUMAN BEHAVIORS form a tripod of warning: bedwetting; playing with fire; harming animals. When they occur together in a child they are strong predictors of pathological personality development—the sort of child that has a risk of developing into a serial killer or an arsonist, for example. Taken singly, any of the behaviors might not predict trouble, but when they cluster something critical may be occurring.

Similarly bears display warning signs that should cause the humans nearby to take note. Bears can become food-conditioned. That is, they can begin to associate the mere presence of human beings with easy sources of food. In some heavily-hiked park areas, for example, bears seem to associate hikers' backpacks with food. Hikers can protect themselves by hiking with food contained in bear-proof canisters, which should reduce the food scents, but this doesn't always work. If the bear has become food-conditioned there doesn't need to be actual food or food scent present for the bear to act as if there is.

Bears can also become habituated. If they come into frequent contact with people they may lose their natural shyness toward us and approach instead of avoid. This can be made worse in an area where there are frequent opportunities for bear/human contact; it seems as if frequent sightings may reduce their sense that we are dangerous and should be left alone.

Bears can exhibit aggressiveness. Despite folklore, adult male bears are much more likely to engage in conflict with people (and with other bears) than are females, even if cubs are present. Smart mother bears send their offspring up a tree to avoid trouble. But one threat even a good-climbing cub can't avoid is an aggressive and hungry male bear. They do sometimes kill and eat cubs. The males' larger sizes mean larger appetites and they are also more likely to attack and kill other young animals—calves, lambs, fawns. Across North America, the black bear is the least aggressive of bears; the polar bear, grizzly, and brown are all more aggressive and also include a larger proportion of meat in their diets.

☆

Even in biblical times, bears were feared and vilified. Bears show up in the Old Testament books of II Kings, I & II Samuel, Isaiah, Ecclesiastes, Hosea, Proverbs, and Lamentations, and the descriptions are threatening—either a warning about a she-bear guarding her cubs, or a more general caution about the bear's ferocity.

The wildest story shows up in II Kings 2:23-25. In these verses, young lads from the city harass and tease the prophet Elisha for his baldness; he curses them in God's name. Immediately two female bears come out of the woods and tear up forty-two of the young men. The prophet goes on his way.

As a clergy daughter, I tiptoe cautiously into the realm of Biblical commentary. There is some suggestion that the number forty-two is an ill omen. It certainly was for the young men. This narrative doesn't appear in many Sunday School lessons, nor in the lectionaries that set out readings for morning worship. No surprise, for the sender of the bears is not the kind and loving father-God that some were taught to believe in. The message seems to be, don't mess with my prophets, or else.

The lads or their offspring (if they lived long enough to have any), may have gotten their revenge over the centuries. The bears in the story, *Ursus arctos syriacus,* Syrian bears, are a sub-species of the European brown bear. In the twentieth century these bears went extinct in Egypt, Israel, Lebanon, and Syria. They still live in Transcaucasia, Iran, Iraq, and Turkey, but no longer inhabit the lands of Elisha.

☆

Actual human fatalities as a result of black bear encounters are rare but they do happen. Since death statistics for black bear-related deaths were first noted in the late 1800s, a total of 65 such human fatalities occurred in North America. (More deaths were attributed to grizzly, brown, or polar bears.) Of the black bear deaths, 35 (54 percent) took place in Canada, 30 (46 percent) in the United States. Most (82 percent) were encounters with bears in the wild as opposed to captive or pet animals. And the victims came from all age groups: adult men (42 percent); children (35 percent); adult women (23 percent).

The numbers also show an increase in fatal interactions beginning in the 1960s. In the '60s and '70s, 18 fatalities occurred, in the '80s and '90s, 19 fatalities occurred, in the years since 2000, 19 fatalities occurred. This increase mirrors growing bear populations and it takes place at a time when the human population was also on the rise and was increasing its habitat—the famous baby boom generation, of which I am a member, pushing ourselves ever outward into suburbia and beyond. It is also quite possible that farther back in time, the reporting and statistics are less reliable—that numbers are skewed and more deaths may have occurred, but were reported anecdotally, in a way not accessible to the data gatherers.

Compared to the Biblical story, 65 deaths over a period of 130 years isn't a shocking toll, compared to 42 in one incident with a balding prophet. But even one death is terrible. And the proportion of children among the victims is sobering. Most of the adult males who died were sportsmen—out in the wilds, hunting or fishing. The children were just in the wrong place at the wrong time, and many were too young to understand, too small to escape. In all cases of reported human fatalities, the bear responsible was tracked and destroyed, an appropriate response to safeguard the public.

This action is too little and too late, according to some. Recently people have begun suing states for not being more proactive regarding potential bear attacks. In Arizona in 1996 Anna Knochel, 16, was attacked and severely mauled by a black bear while working as a counselor at a 4-H camp. She suffered injuries to her head, back, shoulder and one leg, and required multiple surgeries; she survived but remains disabled as a result of the attack. She and her parents sued the state and won sizeable damages, claiming that the bear involved in the attack had already been caught and tagged by state wildlife authorities as a nuisance animal or worse.

Similarly the parents of Samuel Ives, age 11, sued the US Forest Service after a black bear grabbed the boy from his family's tent and killed him in Uinta-Wasatch-Cache National Forest, Utah in 2007. They too won a large award, nearly two million dollars, on the grounds that the bear had caused trouble hours before the fatal attack and there had been no warning from the staff of the National Forest of this bear's presence.

Some people argue that all trouble bears should be put down or relocated to fenced or caged habitats. But what is a trouble bear? An animal that crosses one's land or one that crosses one's path, perhaps. I've had both but haven't felt seriously threatened. And yet my bear has broken into the cottage garage twice, so she's surely losing her fear of humans and is associating our environments with food, two of the three warning strikes. She hasn't hurt anyone and doesn't appear aggressive, but still, she's a worry, one I'm conflicted about. I don't want her to lose her life because she had the poor luck to choose my yard as part of her territory but I also don't want anyone harmed in any way.

☆

For another comparison, the number of highway fatalities in the United States during one year—2010—totaled 32,885. Of these, 31 percent, or 10,228, were due to drunk driving. In Massachusetts alone, in 2009 a total of 334 people died on the highway and 130 of those deaths were attributed to driving under the influence. So in one year, exactly twice as many people died in one small state because of drunk driving as died in 130 years across the entire continent because of bears. Another *sobering* thought.

Accidental death, death before one's natural life span is complete, is always a tragedy. And sometimes it is preventable, which makes it all the more reprehensible. But looking at the numbers, at the deaths due to bears versus the deaths due to drunken humans, it makes one wonder which species ought to be placed, in significant numbers, behind bars or fences.

☆

It's me, Bear . . .

—— Lynn Rogers

☆

faith, hope and . . . jason

IN MANY WAYS, I'm a technosaur. My cell phone is so ancient it is frequently mocked by twelve year olds so I probably won't be chatting on my phone and accidentally walk into a bear. It can't text, but since I don't want to text, no problem. It can't take photos, but most of the phone photos I see are either inappropriate or fuzzy—a real camera works better for me. I use the phone for out of town travel, but when at home, mostly I leave it turned off. Likewise the television. As a writer I value the quiet spaces in life when my brain can spin an idea undisturbed. Being constantly tuned in and available would evaporate those quiet spaces.

I use my computer and laptop daily. My lefty handwriting is so terrible that after twenty-four hours, even I can't translate what I've scribbled down. I compose on the computer and use it extensively to communicate—email is my friend. And I've produced a print magazine on a computer as well as set up websites. I own an electronic book reader which allows me to carry tons of books on a plane without incurring baggage fees. So technology and I have an up and down relationship. But it has its moments . . .

☆

I grew up in a clergy household, so when I hear Faith and Hope, my ear naturally turns to Charity, or in more contemporary translations, Love. Not Jason. But then I'm not in charge of naming baby bears.

I find myself entranced by a small family of wild bears living in the Minnesota forest whose lives are studied by biologist Lynn Rogers. While not tamed, his bears do know the scientist, and when he encounters one in the woods, he calms it with the words, "It's me, Bear . . ." spoken in a deep, calm voice.

Modern technology has made the secret lives of these Minnesota bears visible to the world, myself included. Specifically, a highly engineered and well-managed den cam allows viewing and listening inside the privacy of the winter den of a hibernating black bear.

The family I've grown attached to belongs to Lily, a young female. It includes her first-born cub, Hope, and the younger twins, Faith and Jason, who all live together in an unusual mixed age den described earlier.

Photos and videos and daily reports are archived so that I can view den building, the sleep of hibernation, the actual birth of baby bears and the moment when they first open their eyes. During warm months, the researchers studying these bears follow them with cameras—video and still—so ordinary bear life in the forest is captured as well.

I return again and again to the short clips of bears, exploring, climbing a tree, digging for grubs, and I'm not the only one. Lily and her family have thousands of fans—school children and grandparents, Minnesotans and Californians and Pennsylvanians—folks everywhere have grown attached to this small woods family. There are DVD sets, calendars, mugs, shirts, photographs, even computer mouse pads featuring Lily and her brood. And so when things start to go wrong, everyone worries.

In late May of her first summer, Hope, the firstborn, is abandoned by her mother in a tree. As she is still a nursling, receiving most of her nutrition from her mother, this puts her in grave danger. At some point, the young bear climbs down and disappears. She's gone when the mother returns. For several days the cub is not seen and the mother travels about on her own. The mother bear wears a tracking collar, so her movements can be traced. The cub does not—the collars are too large and too heavy for a cub. So her movements are a mystery.

Also mysterious is the reason for Lily's wandering. She is a young bear and Hope is her first cub. Perhaps she is simply inexperienced and doesn't quite know how to care for her offspring yet. She wouldn't be the first bear mother to abandon a cub.

Finally they are reunited and although the mother's breasts have hardened somewhat, Hope can still nurse. All is well . . . until Lily disappears again, and travels miles from her cub's bedding tree. As this separation continues, researchers place supplemental foods in places where Hope has spent time with her mother. The hungry cub eats but is still emaciated. The drama continues for many days until it becomes clear why Lily has been traveling—she's obeying her body's hormonal instructions. She's in estrus, is seeking mates, and finds willing males.

The cub feeding continues and seems successful. She eats the supplemental foods and also begins to forage on her own. The researchers decide to try a small, light collar so they can keep track of Hope, but the technology isn't sufficient. The GPS signal is too weak to transmit at sufficient distances. Later, they try to adapt a larger, heavier collar for the young cub. Hope resists the collar.

☆

I don't blame her. I too avoid GPS, but it has less to do with a weight about my neck than with other baggage. In my early years I grew up as the only child in a household of three adults, my mother, father, and grandfather—an upside down sort of mixed-age den. My parents, like parents everywhere, were always telling me what to do and what not to do. I felt completely outnumbered and outgunned. As a result,

I developed a strong rebellious streak, which persists to this day. I resist being told what to do and how to do it. While I'm perfectly comfortable instructing others on how *they* should behave, if someone shares such advice with me, the anti-bossing alarm goes off and my back goes up.

GPS does help researchers reach the bears. And thereby it allows me to observe them. So could I obey that bossy, disembodied voice myself? If she says *turn right in fifty yards,* I'd be inclined to share a few choice insults and then turn left. All of which would guarantee that I'd stay in charge, but it wouldn't help me reach my destination.

I admit it: I get lost when driving. But if I study a map in advance and commit the geometry of my route to memory, I do just fine. I also navigate well with a map when my husband drives, even in a country where we don't speak the language or where they drive on the opposite side of the road. Bears too navigate with a map—in their case it's a scent map and they can find their way in the woods with great olfactory sophistication.

☆

Will Lily find her cub again? Eventually they reunite after Lily has mated with at least two males. Together she and Hope begin the fall denning process and during their second winter together, great excitement—Lily gives birth to two new cubs, Jason and Faith. Hope transforms from single cub to big sister. Unfortunately the family will soon shrink. In early April, after the mother leads her three offspring out into the woods, Jason falls behind. He can't keep up with the traveling and is left alone. Faith too provokes concern. While she keeps up with her mother and older sister's travel, she is tiny for a spring cub and the researchers worry about her safety.

Most worries center about Jason, with good reason. In mid April the small male cub dies. This is hard news after watching him scamper up a tree when he first emerged in the spring. Sadness shows on the web pages, in the daily reports, in the photos of the other three bears traveling without him. Because this is a research site, the body is recovered and studied. One of his legs was injured and infected which led to death.

Questions arise. Some fans believe there should have been a rescue, but others criticized the supplemental feeding of Hope during the previous summer. Jason would have required much more intervention. The goal of this long-term research project is to observe and discover how black bears live in the wild. Rescue would interrupt the natural processes, for in the wild, as in our own tamer settings, real life includes death. So nature was allowed to take its course.

In September, trouble returns. Hope disappears. She has been a nervous, skittish bear, startling easily, continuing to resist the tracking collar and paw it off her neck when it grows annoying. The biologists believe her disposition may have been affected by her time alone, hungry and frightened, during her first summer. Whatever the cause, she drops her collar and goes missing. A search ensues and each sighting of a lone young bear is followed up to try to locate this much loved creature.

As days pass, the chances of recovery grow slim. And then, the grim news. Hope has been killed by a hunter. Unbelievable. This charming sister-bear shot.

The researchers in Minnesota work in cooperation with hunters. They believe that judicious hunting can help manage the bear population so that it doesn't grow too large to be tolerated by the human communities nearby. As in Massachusetts, once a limited hunting season was established, the bear population rebounded and is thriving. The hunters return this cooperation by avoiding collared bears, or young bears traveling with a collared mother.

But Hope dropped her collar and took off on her own. In the normal course of bear life, Hope would have already become independent. Lily would have forced her firstborn to leave their home territory during the early summer. The mixed age den might have meant that Hope could stay with her mother and Faith for an extra year. Instead, Lily's family has shrunk to two. Viewers won't get to watch Hope make the transition from cub to mother. Again, sadness pervades the daily reports.

☆

All this bear watching makes me itchy. I need to see my bears again, even though it is winter and they're denned up. Even though they're in Massachusetts and I'm now in Pennsylvania. After seeing clips of bears and of people following bears (walking with bears), I imagine seeking out my bear neighbors in New England. I want to feel the thickness of a bear pelt, follow a mother bear and discover her bedding trees, watch as a cub scrambles up a white pine.

A small voice sits on my shoulder like that annoying GPS tracker and whispers, *bad idea.* I'm not an experienced bear walker. My bears aren't accustomed to being followed and I'd be doing it on my own, without backup, without training. *Really bad idea.* But still . . .

I use that sometimes-friendly technology and send off an e-mail. This summer's bear courses are filled, but next summer's haven't yet started to enroll. So next summer then. I'm going to Minnesota. I'll hang out with bear whisperer Lynn Rogers, and if I'm really lucky I might learn to whisper a bit myself. *It's me, Bear . . .*

. . . life ain't easy for a boy named Sue . . .
—Johnny Cash

a bear named sue

IT'S NOT MINNESOTA, not even the woods. It's more of what Winnie the Pooh might call an *expotition* and it will happen in my own state of Pennsylvania, in my own city of Pittsburgh, at the Pittsburgh Zoo just a couple of miles from my house.

I'm more than a little disappointed. I want to go into the woods, to see wild bears, close up. Minnesota is quite a distance and I'd have to wait till summer, so I've been trying to reach folks at the local game commission without much luck. I've made a contact in Massachusetts but the opportunities for joining or observing a tagging session have diminished there. Maine might work, in mid-March, but that's a long way too and I'm on a deadline. So I arrange a behind-the-ropes visit to the zoo. It will have to do.

I head for the zoo on a chilly gray morning in mid-February. I feel guilty even as I throw on my coat—a leather biker jacket. Is this any way to visit an animal, wearing skin? All my woods-woman gear is stashed in a closet in Massachusetts so I'm stuck with city slick. Yes, I have good strong Sorel boots, but it's about 38 degrees outside and there's no snow. Instead I opt for some old sneakers with good grips on the soles. They can be scrubbed if I step in anything. Wool socks, corduroys and a wool sweater, some fleece mitts and a wool hat. I'll be fine.

Mo Brown is my host, a self-proclaimed tree-hugger, gentle, bearded, soft-spoken. I like him immediately. We sit in a snack bar and get to know each other a bit—he tells bear stories and I explain what I'm hoping for—an intimate encounter with a black bear. Such encounters are everyday news for him—he works especially with the bears and the giraffes, but also helps out with the big cats and the rhinos when needed. He's been a bear guy for many years now and he loves his work. During a spell of illness he needed a lengthy time off to recuperate; once he became ambulatory again, he visited the zoo frequently just to keep connected to his animals. "They respond to my voice," he explains.

A male Andean Spectacled Bear was recently relocated from Pittsburgh to the Phoenix Zoo for breeding purposes. Mo visited him there, and as he spoke to one of the zoo staff near the bear area, the bear approached. Mo could hear him coming, the squish of his paws against the grass. "I don't have especially great hearing or anything," he explains. "But when I'm around the bears they know where I am and I know where they are—we're in communication." This particular bear had been shy in his new habitat, so the Phoenix zoo staff hadn't seen him respond to a friend before. The bear pressed against the fencing to greet Mo, who put his face up close.

"Are you kissing that bear?"

"I am," he replied.

☆

"You'll be meeting Susan for sure. Stanley will probably be sleeping," Mo says.

These are the same bears I visited in the fall. Susan is a small, compact female, about 250 pounds and perhaps five feet tall if standing upright. In the wild she'd be trimmer, maybe about 200, he explains. Stanley is a big male, about 550 pounds. He's lived at the zoo for most of his life, having been orphaned as a cub and brought to

Pittsburgh at about nine months. He may have been a nuisance bear back then, but Mo disdains that label now. Stanley is twenty-eight years old, a calm, mellow old bear.

Susan has lived ⅔ of her life here as his companion. Also orphaned and raised in a rehabilitation facility, she lived in the wild for a time, then came to Pittsburgh at about eight years of age and is now twenty-three. And since the zoo doesn't particularly want any new cubs, Stanley, poor guy, was neutered before Susan's arrival.

All this conversation, of course, heightens my sense of anticipation. And I realize that as we're speaking, Mo is evaluating me—who is this woman and how will she behave with his bears? He tells one final story and it feels a bit like a test. "I was feeding the bears some fruit and sweet potatoes—summer foods. A kid was watching out front and when I left the feeding area, he asked, 'Why are you feeding them fruit? Bears only eat kids.'"

"Where do they get these ideas?," Mo asks. "Can you believe it?"

I shake my head and shrug. Sadly, I can believe just about anything of my fellow humans.

We leave the snack bar and hike up to the bear habitats—mostly rock and cement. He opens a metal gate, then unlocks a dark green door. A little flutter of nerves jangles up my spine.

He leads the way into a narrow, chilly stone and cement hallway intended only for staff. Doorways, openings in the walls are gated, with padlocks. Several bales of straw sit along one side. He guides me carefully up the path. As it was cold last night and the enclosed hallway holds on to the night's chill some spots are icy. We stop at a gate with vertical bars and there she is. Susan.

☆

I was almost named Susan. My parents had narrowed it down to two choices then spent some time with a badly behaving toddler of that name. Which they deemed an omen in favor of Katherine and so Katherine I am. But our son's wife is Susan. One of my close friends has a daughter Susan. So it feels odd to meet Susan the bear. She pokes a curious nose toward me.

Mo greets her with a calm, friendly voice and an ear scratch.

"May I?"

He nods. "She likes to have her ears scratched."

I reach through the bars and scratch the top of her head, caress her velvet ears. Her fur is glossy in the morning light, rough by her nose, softer on top and softest on her ears.

Mo points to her paws and taps a leg. She raises it and he strokes the fur there with one finger. I imitate. The fur atop her paw is very rough—lots of guard hairs—and her claws are long and black. The underside of her paw shows black skin.

My hand is inside the bar and yet it takes a few minutes for my mind to catch up. I am actually petting a full-grown black bear. She sniffs me and seems as interested in me as I am in her.

Mo turns to retrieve a plastic bag and begins to offer her some prunes. She laps them up neatly. Then he places some in my hand. I extend my hand flat, as if feeding apple slices to a horse, and offer her one sticky prune at a time. Her tongue is warm and wet. It reminds me of my friends' various dogs, of the calves' tongues at the dairy farm, but hers is less rough than the calves'. And muscular, agile—she flips the prunes into her mouth without a sign of teeth, for which I'm grateful.

Mo switches to dried cranberries, a red handful. Susan is a delicate eater. She flicks a small bunch in and then another.

He places cranberries in my hand and I hold it out to her. One lick, two licks, three. One lone cranberry remains on my palm, and her tongue snakes out and captures it. For such a large animal, she can even sense a half-inch berry on someone else's hand.

We visit for a spell, until the cranberries are gone. My hands are sticky, mostly from the fruit, but also from bear spit. I continue stroking her strong head, her soft ears, her pointed muzzle. I look into her dark eyes and she returns my gaze. I'm sure I'm smiling and I hope she is too, however it is that a bear smiles. And though it is against the zoo's regulations, I wish I could sneak behind her gate, give her a people hug and receive a bear hug in return.

As we ready ourselves to leave, Mo leans down and goes nose to nose with this bear. He is saying goodbye to one of his close friends.

As we exit the hallway and return to the public viewing area, I notice a chill, partly from the cold, hard surfaces, partly from exposure to the wind. And a raucous squawking greets us—some big bird. Turns out to be Van Gogh—a large male peacock who also likes the dried cranberries he finds on the sidewalk. His call sounds to me like *hel-low* and so I return it. We *hel-low* back and forth for a while and I notice the fine mist of his breath in the air each time he squawks. To be this close, to see the winter breath of an animal as clearly as I see my own—it's a surprise, an unexpected gift.

I turn and watch Susan the bear as she returns to her habitat.

She watches me right back.

"Goodbye," I call. "Goodbye, Susan."

Mo nods, as if he approves, and I stuff my chilly hands into my pockets and head down the path, toward the car and home.

acknowledgments

This book began oddly. I was reading a collection of lyrical essays by nature writer, Barbara Hurd in preparation for a conference on *The Essay*. Immediately after I finished *Walking the Wrack Line*, it felt as though my hands had developed a mind of their own. I turned on the computer without intending to and began to type—about bears.

A few weeks later as I attended the conference, I heard Barbara Hurd speak and was fortunate to attend a small group workshop that she led. Many of her words resonated, but perhaps the most powerful was her answer to a student question.

"How do you know when a book is finished?"

"When I stop obsessing about it," she replied.

I recognized myself in those words; I was obsessed with bears and wanted to work on nothing else. So I wrote about bears for months. My first thanks, then, go to Barbara, for her inspiration, for sharing her thoughts on the construction of braided essays, and for permission to obsess. Secondly, thanks go to Chatham University for sponsoring the conference, and in particular to Sheryl St. Germain who directs the MFA program there where I am fortunate to teach. And a big shout-out to everyone at Autumn House Press for making this book a reality: to Michael Simms for his energy and excitement, and to Caroline Tanski, who has been a most gracious editor throughout.

Along the way, I've been grateful for my writers' group: Sally Alexander, Jackie Robb, Sharon Flake, Lee McClain, Betty Howard, Dick and Pat Easton, Jonathan Auxier, and Colleen McKenna. They have encouraged me every time I shared an essay and urged me to stretch, to write more and more, as have more distant friends, Karen Williams and Regina Brennan. Thanks, too, to Amy Cush who has offered fresh ideas and to Diane French who forwarded lots of wild photos.

I've also appreciated the myriad resources available: various state departments of natural resources, departments of fisheries and wildlife, the Pittsburgh Zoo and Aquarium. And of course, to Mo Brown, the Pittsburgh Zoo's bear whisperer. Thanks too, to the bear researchers who share their results freely in both print and online media, and to the people who have opinions about bears, whether positive or negative. To the hunters and anti-hunters, to those who see bears as dangerous and those who see them as shy.

I tried, as I wrote these essays, to present as much information as I could, and to present it in my own terms. What you see on these pages is not a manifesto, nor a field study. It is not pro- or anti-anything in particular; I hope it follows no party line, represents no lobbying group. It is simply, in the best words I could find, one woman's response to bears.

Throughout the project, I've counted on the support and kindness of my family—they have provided some of the stories in the essays, and I hope I've portrayed them honestly. In particular, my husband Russ has listened to endless tales of bears and put up with a highly distracted partner for months on end. Many, many thanks.

But the biggest thank you of all goes to the black bears—the ones who have wandered into my yard and into my imagination. May you live long and prosper.

The Autumn House Nonfiction Series

Michael Simms, General Editor

design and production

Cover and text design: Chiquita Babb
Cover photographs: iStockphoto
Author photograph: Russ Ayres
Text set in Perpetua, a font designed by Eric Gill in 1925
Printed by McNaughton & Gunn on 55# Glatfelter Natural